T0090424

Gaijin Teacher; Foreign Sensei

Bill Weeks

Order this book online at www.trafford.com
or email orders@trafford.com

Most Trafford titles are also available at major online book retailers.

Printed in Victoria, BC, Canada.

ISBN: 978-1-4269-3123-9 (sc)
ISBN: 978-1-4269-3124-6 (dj)
ISBN: 978-1-4269-3125-3 (e-book)

Library of Congress Control Number: 2010905779

*Our mission is to efficiently provide the world's finest, most comprehensive book publishing
service, enabling every author to experience success. To find out how to publish your book, your
way, and have it available worldwide, visit us online at www.trafford.com*

Trafford rev. 05/12/2010

Trafford
PUBLISHING® www.trafford.com

North America & international
toll-free: 1 888 232 4444 (USA & Canada)
phone: 250 383 6864 ♦ fax: 812 355 4082

In loving memory of Paul Weeks
who took a stand on civil rights
when the issue was still in doubt.

With thanks to

Michiko Schricker and Yumiko Weeks

Contents

There is a giant in the Japans that sits unfazed by events around it. It has sat like a giant rocky jizo-sama as a typhoon buffeted castles and village huts alike, drenching the countryside and sending hopes and aspirations flying and shattering like bamboo mats in a storm. It watched earthquakes rock giant freeway structures back and forth like a pendulum until they fell and crushed terrified commuters below. For centuries tsunamis have swelled, crested, and poured into coastal towns pounding and ripping up all in their paths until the waters and screams subsided...without the giant so much as raising an eyebrow.

Kanagawa fishermen, soaked to the skin, wide-eyed and with hearts pounding, have feverishly stroked their oars in battle with murderous seas. But between the great wave crests, the giant sat quietly watching detached and unmoved. The giant holds a surprise that will dwarf all the meaningful-meaningless events that take place from time to time around it.

Snow can fall on the volcano giant known as Fujisan any month out of the year. Eventually it melts and wends its way along lava tubes and pumice, seeping through soil on a five year journey until reappearing at the surface near Numazu, and flowing into the Kanagawa River and eventually on into Suruga Bay.

Fujisan watched battles where armor clad samurai fought and bled and died for reasons the farmer who now floods the rice paddy and plants on that land can not say. Fujisan was there when the 17 year old Musashi fought on the losing side of his first battle, at

Sekigahara, that led to the establishment of the first shogunate. More than 10,000 men were left dead or dying in October of 1600, but Musashi escaped to become the most famous swordsman in Japanese history; a swordsman almost as remarkable with his artist's brush as with his sword.

It is no wonder that the ancient Shinto practicing inhabitants respected and worshipped the great giant as well as waterfalls and lakes. It is also no wonder that they adapted the ways of Buddhism which came from India by way of China and Korea partly out of a respect for the attributes of that religion that are exhibited by the mountain. Like some of the natives in the Americas who combined their ancient natural beliefs with the Christian religion, many Japanese today still practice both Shintoism and Buddhism.

In a year supposedly 2000 years after the birth of the fisher of men, and precisely two months shy of the four hundredth anniversary of the battle of Sekigahara, Will Mast and Yumiko Hirota had their second wedding ceremony. It was at the Gotemba Kogen Hotel, located on an ancient lava flow, near the base of Fujisan.

The Gotemba Kogen is a beautiful resort. It has both traditional and modern, western-style rooms, a luxurious onsen, a great German restaurant, yurts for karaoke, and ancient, huge cherry trees famous for the Gotemba city flower, sakura (cherry blossoms).

Someday the walls will ignite and the windows will melt and run like streams from intense heat seconds before glowing lava knocks down and consumes what is left of the beautiful Gotemba-Kogen Hotel. Without a doubt this will happen when Fujisan awakens again, sometime before Ayla Michaela Mast's child (Maeven Alexandra Bixby born in March 2010) becomes as old as Ayla's Grandma Ruth is today.

Then, two to three hundred years after that, the giant will annihilate the next collection of hopes and dreams that anyone dares to build anywhere in its path. No one will be able to stop it. The giant will yawn and go back to sleeping and waiting as unconcerned with the next generation as it is with you or me or any of the saints and sinners living in its shadow some of whose stories are found in the next pages.

Businessman's Poem

Suzuki Kentaro, or, as English-speakers would say, Kentaro Suzuki, had dropped by his company in the Ginza district of Tokyo briefly that morning. No one questioned the actions of the president who was dressed in a dark business suit as he rummaged through a few files, found what he was looking for, exited and climbed into the luxury Toyota he had bought just before business began to drop off a few years earlier.

As Suzuki-san entered the Tomei Toll highway, headed south, Akihiro Hirota had already been at work in the family restaurant in Gotemba, cleaning and slicing fresh eel. He was not entirely happy with his youngest daughter, Yumiko's choice of the American teacher Will Mast for her husband. On the other hand, she was closer to 40 than 30 and the only one of his four children who had never married.

Akihiro-san adjusted the bandana on his head, and thought about his wife, Koto, who had been killed by a hit and run driver many years earlier. He wondered what she would have thought of her baby's choice and this new turn of events.

Akihiro-san blinked his thick, wrinkled eyes rapidly, then looked around to make sure none of the help had come in yet and seen him. He was in his early 70's yet seldom missed a day of work. He was expecting his daughter, Sanae, and employee and friend of the family, Aka-chan (Baby), his granddaughter (Sanae's daughter), Oryo, her foreign husband, George Olsen and their children (his great grandchildren), Mariko and Hiroshi. After all, George, who did not speak with a southern accent even though he hailed from Alabama, had turned out pretty well. He had a good job with a prestigious English school that catered to well-to-do companies. George spoke fluent Japanese, and seemed to appreciate Japanese culture more than some Japanese high school students did. Maybe this California teacher marrying Yumiko would not be so bad. Maybe.

There were two Hirota eel restaurants. The first, situated in Minami-Gotemba, he had turned over to first son, Ryoma, who lived with his wife in the house in back. They still used the same secret eel sauce that had been in the family for generations. The restaurant was popular with the in-crowd, from young salary men to the politicians of several near by towns.

This second Hirota's sat on the second floor of a small bunch of shops and restaurants, a few blocks from the Gotemba eki (train station). This one had its ups and downs, struggling a bit more with a fickle public, though there were several "regulars" who would come for lunch or dinner two or three times a week.

Akihiro-san had washed down the outside with a hose before turning to his eel preparation chores in the kitchen. There were two rooms with booths and tatami mats on which patrons could sit, a counter by the kitchen with a television at one end, and in the center of the room a four-cornered counter to sit at.

Inside that were an iriori "fire" with red chili peppers as flames and a traditional pot with an iron fish perched above it, on a long metal pole.

On the wall hung an old traditional straw rain coat, hat, and straw boots. There were signed pictures of Tokyo Giants and Yakult Swallows baseball players, and a picture of an American actor with English writing saying, "To Hirota-san. Thanks for the most oishi meal I had in Gotemba. Richard Gere." A statue of a large raccoon-dog with enormous testicles stood guard outside by the entrance.

Suddenly the door slid to one side and one flap of the noren rose up. "mastah! otosan? doko desuka?"

It was Itsuki, his second son, who owned two drinking restaurants, Kinkabu I in Iwanami and Kinkabu II in Gotemba, a few blocks away.

"nanda?" the old man grunted in reply.

"ohayo gozaimasu."

"ohayo. juugyooinwa kiteinainoka?" ("Doesn't anyone work any more?")

"himanandesu. ("Business is slow.") "chotto yotte, tetsudaidemo shiteikookanato omotte." ("I thought I would drop by and give you a hand.")

The old man considered this for a moment. He wondered what the visit was really about. He searched the face of his son. "darega junbishiterunda?" ("Who is doing your prep?")

Itsuki dodged the question. "daijoobudesuyo." ("It's covered,") he said off-handedly. " jooji kuru?" ("George coming by?")

Now things became clearer. "aa, atodena. Oryoto kodomo mo isshoni. mata konpyuutaano chooshiga waruinoka?" ("Later, along with Oryo and the kids. You having trouble with your computer again?")

"sonnakotowa naiyo. ("No trouble,") Itsuki lied. "chotto kikitaikotoga arudake. ("Just need a little advice is all.")

Akihiro-san indicated another knife with his head. Itsuki took it and picked up a still-squirming eel from a bucket writhing with fish. The two of them worked through the morning.

They talked about business and sports. Akihiro-san thought Kinkabu II's new second cook might work out well, but he questioned leaving Kinkabu I in the hands of an incompetent like Yasunobu.

"ano wakazoodewa, okyakuga konakunatteshimau. okyakuttenowa, oishiimonwa sugu wasureteshimau." ("That youngster will drive customers away. People will forget about a great meal in no time,") "demo mazuimon tabesaseraretara, moo nidoto kitekurenai."("But a disaster they will remember forever.") he said chopping a fish in half for emphasis.

Itsuki let the remark slide, and wondered what the chances of the Yakult Swallows were against the Tokyo Giants that year. Both men were Swallows fans, but Akihiro-san always praised the giants in front of customers since most of them were Giants fans. He kept a large cask of sake by the entrance, along with a pile of square wooden sake cups—a gift to his customers no matter which team won.

Aka-chan and Sanae showed up an hour later and set up their stations.

Aka-chan had been working at Hirota's off and on for years. She had been a friend of the family even longer. Small, thin, with short hair (occasionally dyed red), her real name was Akashio, but somewhere along the line her name turned into "Baby" (Aka-chan). She worked hard at Hirota's, serving, cleaning, and generally doing anything that needed to be done. Servers don't receive tips in Japan, which means the pay is even more important. Aka-chan often held down two or sometimes even three jobs to make ends meet (working in the kitchen of a private golf club as well).

Despite her struggle, she managed to live at the same Gotemba Chateau where Yumiko and Will lived, along with the most important thing in her life, her son, Bisaku.

Bisaku stood almost a head taller than his mother and had a splash of blonde dyed hair at the front of his head (a source of constant irritation to Akihiro-san). Baby had scrimped and saved in order to put Bisaku through the prestigious Nakamura School's English Immersion program nearly from the time it first began. Bisaku was keenly aware of his mother's sacrifices for him, but he was no scholar. As soon as his mother dropped him off at the train station he would lower his pants like many of the other boys. He would joke around at school, and sometimes take a furtive break to have a smoke.

Once the school administration approached Aka-chan about moving her son over from the immersion program to the less-expensive, regular program. Much to Bisaku's chagrin, Aka-chan would have none of it. She knew he would have a better education on the immersion side.

He would be graduating from high school in a couple years, and spent most of his free time studying for a battery of tests that would be the major determination of the kind of career in which he would wind up. When not studying he played computer or phone games or thought about girls.

When Aka-chan happened to see him and he was playing one of the phone games, he would look away with a feeling of deep guilt. He would think of the last practice test he had taken at Kumon and how the teacher had ridiculed him. He knew how hard his mother worked, and a deep sense of shame would come over him.

"jikanbakka mudani shite... dooshite motto shikkari benkyoshitekurenaino?" ("Why do you waste your precious time?") she would ask, real sorrow in her voice.

He would put his phone away without replying and feign indifference. But he would scratch his face or pick at his acne, a practice that seemed to grow more and more as time and pressure built. It seemed to Akihiro-san that every time he saw the boy he had more facial scars than the last time.

Sanae was Akihiro's eldest, Yumiko's older sister by 12 years. She had been married and divorced, and had two daughters (both married). Always pleasant and smiling, she worked hard as a waitress/cashier/ manager/ and accountant for Hirota's in Gotemba. She had recently been in the process of moving from her comfortable home in Gotemba, with her English sheep dog, Gray, to a new home in Jurigi on the side of Mt. Fuji.

She came in, gave her greetings, put away her personal items, and went about tidying the restaurant.

George and Oryo and their kids arrived soon after that. Oryo would bus tables later, while Mariko and little Hiroshi chased a cat trying to use the raked Zen garden outside for a toilet. By the time the first customers came in Itsuki and George were sitting at the counter near the television with both George and Itsuki's computers (Itsuki's computer just happening to have been in his car), jabbering back and forth in English and Japanese, working on a new program that had been giving Itsuki problems.

Akihiro-san shook his head. "naniga konpyuutaada. kireena koiya chakio nagameruhooga doredake iika." ("Damn computers. Never saw one half as interesting as a graceful koi or a well-crafted tea cup.")

x x x x x x x x x x x x x x x x x x x x x x

It was getting close to two hours since he had left home that morning when Kentaro Suzuki pulled off the Tomei at the Gotemba exit and paid his toll. He was not interested by the many "love motels" within the first few blocks, and hardly noticed the Pachinko parlor. On the main street there was a Shinto temple where a woman kannushi presided. He considered stopping briefly but instead pulled over to a stationery store. There he purchased thick paper imbedded with flower petals, and a shodo-style brush and ink set. He asked where he could find the best unagi in town, and was directed to the Gotemba Hirota's.

Sanae-san brought the polite gentleman in the dark business suit a small bowl of kimosui, broth with an eel's heart in the bottom. She then brought an unaju, rectangular shellacked box lined with four fillets of eel atop a bed of rice and cooked in the wonderful sauce for which the restaurant was known. She poured and later repoured sake for him from a small tokeri.

When finished, Sanae asked if he would care to purchase a bottle of shochu with his name written on it in gold that he could use whenever he returned. He politely declined, but asked if he could continue to sit at the booth while he did some work. The restaurant was not crowded and Sanae was quick to assure him that he could stay as long as he liked, clearing his dishes and wiping the space before him with a dry cloth.

Kentaro Suzuki opened a briefcase and took out the shodo set. He asked for water and dabbled some on the ink block where he mixed it in small circles. He knew how he wanted to begin, but wasn't sure of the ending. He dabbed the brush in the ink, and deftly began writing kanji characters on the thick paper.

Mariko and Hiroshi had been playing outside the restaurant for quite some time. Hiroshi came inside and saw the quiet, strange man in the expensive suit and peered shyly around the corner at him. The man smiled and played a game of peek-a-boo using his hands in front of his face. Hiroshi pulled back quickly, but smiled in spite of himself. He peered around the corner again, his eyes dancing with joy at the attention he was receiving. Mariko opened the door and a breeze entered, tousling Hiroshi's hair and distracting him from the game.

Kentaro Suzuki's eyes opened ever so slightly as he recognized the divine intervention. He knew now how to finish his poem. He deftly began to paint with his shodo brush.

> Sweet turned sour, my coming and going
> Mixed up as leaves blown by a fan
> Fujisan's wind

He then politely asked for directions to the Sea of Trees.

Itsuki explained that he was on the wrong side of Mt. Fuji. He gave him directions north to Highway 138 and 139, past the bridge that crosses over to the amazing Ichiku Kubota Kimono Museum, past the doll museum, and on past Fujinomiya and the rest of the Five Lakes.

Kentaro Suzuki thanked him. He left a ¥10,000 note and said the change was to buy something for the children as they had done him a great service. Then he followed the directions to Aokigahara. He parked his car and placed the poem on the dashboard next to apologies to his family and employees for having failed them. He marked his way through the rustling trees with yellow ribbon tape to help in finding his body, slit the veins in his wrists, and watched his life spill onto the leaves of the forest floor.

Second Wedding

For instance, to an American it might seem rude to bring money instead of a gift to a wedding. If they did find their way past that, they'd sure as hell demand a way to keep check on who was collecting the money, or at least get a receipt for tax purposes or something.

Yet here were intelligent people, some with whom Will Mast had never exchanged a word in his life, bringing ¥50,000 or more per couple, handing it over in elaborate envelopes with ties or string bows adorning them, to a couple of young ladies who bowed and wrote down how much they brought. They then followed the haunting sounds of koto strings being plucked, floating through the lobby from the convention hall of the Gotemba Kogen Hotel near Fujioka. A large sign read "INFORMATION" in English, but all the small print below was in Japanese, except for the table names which were American states…. in English.

Although the Japanese bubble economy had burst ten years before, many of the guests arrived in Mercedes or other fancy cars, dressed in their finest. Perhaps half the women wore colorful kimonos, and even some of the men had on kimonos as well.

"Hello, Will," it was Fukumoto-san wearing a stunning traditional brown kimono. Keiko-san, his wife, was on one arm and a beautiful, young blonde girl, (Will's daughter by a previous marriage)—was on his other.

"You're lookin' good, dad," said Ayla Michaela Mast.

"Thanks to Fukumoto-san," Will said, smiling. It was Fukumoto-san who had lent him the fancy wedding kimono he wore, except for the white stockings and geda. "Better grab your seats. You're on California."

Each round table held a small pedestal in its center with the name of a U.S. state. There was Will's state, California; Colorado where Yumiko liked to take people for home visits; and Alabama, from where George, who was married to Yumiko's niece, Oryo, hailed. There were a few other states like Hawaii who were there just because Yumiko liked their names.

A young but competent woman emcee with stylish, short hair checked her notes once more as guests found their name cards. Laminated photo collages of the honeymoon on Catalina Island, California, and of the first wedding ceremony in Ramona served as placemats. Gifts of Native American dream-catchers and ornate blue ceramic Japanese serving bowls (meticulously wrapped, of course) were removed from the chairs as guests seated themselves.

The young emcee leaned into her microphone. "Minasama, gochakusekikudasaimase." ("Everyone please take your seats.")

The lights dimmed. It was time for Will to enter and make his way alone to the center of the room. He checked the obi (sash) of his kimono, and tried not to clank too loudly with the wooden cross bars of his geda (sandals) which raised him yet another inch or so above much of the crowd.

"How the hell did I ever get here?" he thought.

As he walked in the darkened room, he could just make out Fukumoto, Keiko and Ayla again sitting at the California table, Ayla's long blonde hair a stand out in the mostly dark haired crowd. It was partly because of his daughter, Ayla, that Will, a San Onofre, California surfer turned teacher, now found himself in this unlikely situation. He had accompanied her to Japan five years earlier when her modeling agency, Elan, had sent her at the tender age of fifteen, to spend the summer doing print jobs, runway modeling and other fashion work. The drivers used to laugh when she tried to get into the wrong side of the company car. "Are you driving, Ayra Michaera?" they would ask. He had also heard about her dancing and drinking in Roppongi after he had returned to the U.S. to teach summer school, about her falling into a fountain, and about the Japanese girls in a bar who imitated the bizarre hairstyle she had created on a whim once by wrapping rubber bands around tufts of her hair.

It was on that first trip where he met Emiko Watanabe, a teacher at a school located along the old cedar lined foot path Tomei section in Hakone, who had asked him if an English teacher friend of hers could visit his class back in Long Beach to see how English was taught to young native speakers.

"My pleasure," he said.

But it was more than just a pleasure. From the moment he set eyes on Yumiko Hirota in the hallway of Truman Elementary in Long Beach, her slight, Audrey Hepburn frame bending down to get a better view of the students' work in the hall. As she turned and saw him, her face beamed a smile as she guessed he was the one with whom she had spoken on the phone—first long distance from Gotemba, Japan, and then the night before from her hotel room on the Queen Mary permanently berthed in Long Beach Harbor.

They couldn't get enough of one another after that. He took her to lunch at Pancho's, a small Mexican restaurant, and at Frenchy's Bistro, both around the corner from the school. Yumiko changed her itinerary in order to spend almost two weeks studying the way English was taught in American elementary classrooms—and also just happened to join Will in catching Doug MacLeod's blues at The Blue Café, jazz at Spaghetini's, and even belly dancing over flaming cheese appetizers and retsina at Mykonos on Long Beach's 2nd Street Strip.

There were several other trips to the US by Yumiko after that—sometimes to study the way English was taught in American schools, and sometimes to guide her own groups of English learners who came to do home stays in Colorado and California. Somehow she always managed to get Long Beach on the itinerary. There were also lots of long distance phone calls in between visits which sometimes lasted for hours. It was during one of those phone calls Will decided he had been single long enough (he'd been divorced from Ayla's mother for fifteen years), and proposed.

Yumiko's normal talkativeness left her, and there was a silence for a long time. "Are you sure that's what you want?"

"Absolutely."

"Then I accept," she said simply.

When you marry someone from another country, it is akin to marrying the whole country. Now when Will rooted for teams in the Olympics, he found himself rooting for the US team and the Japanese team. If the teams played each other it was hard to know which one to root for sometimes. Will knew that although his favorite baseball team was always the Dodgers, he now liked the Yakult Swallows as well. In fact, his favorite US major league player became a player from Japan—Ichiro Suzuki. He was the most exciting player he'd ever seen. He could hit anything (later setting a new record for most hits in a season—and another for most seasons batting over 300). Will once saw him get a base hit off a wild pitch that had hit the dirt before coming to the plate. Another time he fielded a ball in right field and threw a runner out at third base. Ichiro had made Will a Mariners fan as well.

After their decision to marry, Will made another trip to Japan—to meet the family. Yumiko's mother had been hit and killed by a car earlier. Her father, Akihiro-san, ran Hirota's in Gotemba, a traditional Japanese style restaurant specializing in eel. Her oldest brother, Ryoma, ran another Hirota eel restaurant in neighboring Minami-Gotemba, while her younger brother, Itsuki, ran two successful drinking establishments, Kinkabu I and Kinkabu II (named for his three daughters), one in Inami, and the other also in Gotemba. Yumiko's older sister, Sanae, worked in Akihiro-san's restaurant doing a bit of everything.

Yumiko's brothers had treated Will warmly. These were no "inscrutable Orientals." Instead they reminded Will more of the family-centered Mexican Americans he had spent so much time with in California. Their greatly loved but spoiled children climbed all over his lap and shoulders at family gatherings. Wives, Atsuko and Yuki, and sister Sanae, kept food and drink coming continuously. They had dinners in Will's honor, demanded speeches which no one understood, toasted "kampai" relentlessly, and even insisted on taking

Will to karaoke. Itsuki always sang his renditions of "Country Roads" and "San Francisco", mostly out of tune.

Yumiko's father, Hirota Akihiro, was a different matter. He stood behind Hirota's glass counter filled with sashimi, sliding chunky bits of chicken onto a wooden skewer for yakitori, and glowered at Will from under his headband. Every now and then he would surprise Will with a bit of English. "You nevah, nevah hit Yumiko."

Will shook his head in surprise, "Oh no."

"No?!" questioned old man Hirota, starting to redden. "NO??!" And he slammed the meat laden skewer to the counter.

Will learned later that in Japan a negative is agreed to positively. He should have said "Yes", meaning, "Yes, I'll nevah hit her", rather than the American way of "No, I won't hit her,"—but at the time he could only wonder what the elderly Akihiro Hirota was upset about.

"You want me to hit her?" he asked, bewildered.

"I kendo you," Akihiro-san shouted. He held up several thick fingers. "Three degree." He reached towards a thick wooden stick leaning against the wall, next to an old fashioned straw rain coat and boots.

Will's eyes widened. Just then Yumiko returned to the counter where he was sitting. It was her habit to get up and help out now and then around the restaurant, especially if they were busy. "What's wrong?" she asked.

"Your dad thinks I want to hit you," Will said.

"Why do you want to hit me?" she frowned. "What kind of man you are?" (She always transposed the you with the are when asking a question). "<u>You</u> are not American."

"I don't want to hit anybody. All I want to do is eat my.....whatever it is I'm eating." The comment was strange in that the only food he was holding was a bowl of rice, but he had been exposed to many new foods lately. Will reached for some soy sauce and splashed some in the bowl.

Yumiko shrieked. Hirota-san slammed his fist down so hard Will thought the counter would break. Sanae, who was walking past carrying dishes, laughed out loud.

"Now what?" Will was sure they had all gone mad.

Yumiko grabbed his dish away. "Murderer. You ruined it," she said, taking the bowl.

"Ruined what?"

"The rice, of course. I must teach you how to eat."

Old man Hirota threw the rice out, and produced a new, steaming bowl full of rice.

"I always put soy sauce on my rice." Will grabbed the bowl from the counter. "I've been eating rice since before you were born. <u>You</u>," he said, pointing the chopsticks at Yumiko, " don't have to teach <u>me</u>," pointing back at himself, "anything about eating." His actions produced another shriek and something sounding like curses in Japanese punctuated with "baka gaigin" from behind the counter.

"Now what? That's it. I give up. I'm not hungry anymore." Will crammed the chop sticks into the rice and set the bowl down. Then, feeling his actions called for him to do more, he pushed his way out through the nori hanging in front of the door.

Immediately he realized he had over-reacted, and, worse, he didn't have anywhere to go. He walked around for a minute or two, looked down the street, knew his limited Japanese wouldn't even produce a conversation with a stranger, then came limping back into the restaurant.

It wasn't until several weeks later that he was able to piece together the various faux pas he committed that night. For some reason known only to the ever-looming Fujisan, it's a sin to spoil rice with soy sauce and it's terribly rude to point with chop sticks. It also turns out that chop sticks are left stuck in rice only at funerals. Will's saying no when he should have said yes was the least of his transgressions.

That's one of many things he smiled to himself about now, standing in the huge room, waiting for his next adventure since his alliance with the fascinating Ms. Hirota.

The lights in the ballroom went down, and a battery of spotlights began waving around from several directions effectively managing to blind him. It was time for Yumiko's grand entrance.

Some of the spotlights traveled over to the doors on one side of the room. The doors parted, and two young girls looking more like dolls dressed in kimonos than children, led the way. They were followed by Yumiko and her father, doing a curious halting step the same way they had done during the wedding in California. It had cost more than 100,000 yen just to rent Yumiko's wedding kimono, which came with a dresser who also did her elaborate hairdo, the hair sticking out in a bizarre Bride of Frankenstein fashion and tilted to one side.

"Now I am really dressed up to the nines," she had beamed.

Her skin looked soft and radiant. Will remembered how he had sat in a chair in a barber shop section of Numazu a few days earlier, getting a haircut. Yumiko was in the next chair...getting a shave. The barber spent a long time shaving her chin, cheeks, and the nape of her neck. It was the first time Will ever saw a woman in shaving lather.

The entourage wound its way through the tables and ended in the middle of the floor. Akihiro Hirota-san gave Will Yumiko's hand, and managed a smile. The couple turned and walked to a small stage where their table was raised for all to see. Will ate almost everything. Yumiko didn't touch a bite.

The emcee gave a brief biography of each of them, and told how they met. She explained the phone proposal, and a trip along the coast to Big Sur during Will's school's winter break. They had continued up the jagged coastline to Santa Cruz, where, on First Night, he presented her with an engagement ring that had belonged to his mother.

After that several people sang for them. Yumiko's singing teacher did something from an opera, and some of her school chums did a popular favorite (roughly translated as "I Am Not Alone")—in which Yumiko joined them. Mr. Yamagiwa did a gracious toast and speech (though Will didn't understand a word of it). While the food was brought out, the lights dimmed and the guests munched while a video was shown of the wedding in California. Yumiko and Will snuck out, took an elevator to their room, and changed out of their kimonos. Yumiko got into the same wedding off-white gown she had ordered made for the Ramona wedding, (based on one she had seen in the movie, *Father of the Bride*), and Will into a tuxedo (a $500 rental in Japan).

Will snuck in and back to the center of the room. The lights went all the way down and spotlights came up waggling around blinding people until they focused on the same door they had illumined earlier. When it opened, the same two cherubs came out—this time decked out in pale blue and pink diaphanous western gowns Grandma Ruth had sent from Ramona, California and carrying small baskets from which they threw hydrangea petals Yumiko and Will had gathered a day or two earlier on the hills between Gotemba and Hakone.

Yumiko's father handed her over once again. There was more singing and speeches, including a very short one Will made in Japanese, which brought a lot of laughter. People came up and poured beer and sake for the couple. At first Will tried to keep up with them, downing the drinks as best he could. Eventually he gave up, only taking a sip or two after each new toast...and soon there were dozens of half-filled glasses littering the top of the table.

Yumiko never touched a drop nor ate a crumb the whole time, but smiled and fretted continuously over everything. Now and then she would explain what was being said, or something Will should do.

After awhile, she took off again—leaving Will to eat and drink, and say "arigatoo" as more drinks and toasts were offered. In about fifteen or twenty minutes she was back, this time wearing a completely new, bright blue gown.

Will leaned over, "Uh, how many dresses are you going to wear?"

"Just one more after this," she said. "I have a special one for the after party party."

Near the end of the evening, Yumiko presented her father with one of the clay dolls she had spent months making at her clay doll class. It was dressed like a prairie frontier woman from the old U.S. west, bending to collect flowers. There wasn't a dry eye.

Except for Fujisan— who never blinked.

Ramona (back in June)

"It won't last."

It was Walt, Will's brother, almost twelve years older than him, calling from the Ramona Estates Guest Houses a mile down the road where he was staying to attend the wedding.

"East is East and West is West."

Walt had a fetish about things western. He liked to wear cowboy boots and hats—and was forever listening to the twanging sounds of country music. He had several books describing brands used on cattle in the old days of the west, and even had a nice collection of branding irons himself along a wall, on top of a book case and on his fire place mantel. He was always telling Will about different brands from different "spreads" which he wanted to acquire for his collection.

"I was hoping you'd fly over to Gotemba for the second ceremony and reception," Will had said into the phone at Mom Ruth's house where the ceremony would take place.

"Couldn't," said Walt, swigging a Budweiser. "I'd starve to death."

"Are you kidding? They own four restaurants over there. The food is great."

Walt rolled his eyes and scratched himself with a hand adorned with a large turquoise stone ring. He glanced through the curtains of his room towards the immaculate golf course. "If they're too lazy to cook it," he drawled in his phony Texan accent, "I'm too lazy to eat it." "Besides," he added, "this boy don't bow to nobody no how, not even the Japanese president."

"Prime Minister. Just be careful what you say when our Japanese guests arrive."

There were eleven of them flying in the next day to attend the wedding, including Yumiko's father, oldest brother, sister, niece, and several family friends with a mountain of luggage. Will was renting a large twelve passenger van to pick them all up at the Los Angeles airport, and bring them down to Ramona, a small California town Northeast of San Diego between Escondido and Julian. Will and Walt's parents were both divorced and remarried, and their mother, Ruth, now eighty years old, was holding the wedding at her home in the Ramona Estates. She and her new husband, Dick, had over a thousand rose plants in their yard, which they pruned, weeded and other wise cared for day after day. At night they would often go round dancing.

Yumiko wanted to go to a grocery store to pick up a few items to give to her brother and sister to take back to Japan. That's right, a grocery store where she could get authentic American food items. Yumiko was already beginning to combine traditional American foods with Japanese foods, something that would lead to her writing *Yumi's Yummies*, an American/Japanese fusion cookbook, several years later.

Will drove Yumiko down to the local Albertsons. He brought a list of items Mother Ruth (Grandma Ruth when Ayla Michaela was around), asked Will to pick up for snack food and last minute guest pleasers. Once at the store, Yumiko and Will went their separate ways to shop.

Will had just rounded up all but the last item on his list, when he noticed a lanky, young stock boy standing in an aisle next to Yumiko, his face bright red. Will continued to pass by, but something nagged at him just enough that he decided he had better find out what was going on.

"Is there anything wrong, Sweetie?"

"Oh no," smiled Yumiko brightly. "I'm just getting some help finding things."

Will nodded and turned to move on, but something about the boy's expression made him turn back again. He looked questioningly at him.

The boy seemed to be picking his words carefully. "I think she may want a drugstore." His eyes went down, and his voice got softer, "...or maybe further down the street.." (very softly now)... "to the...uh... adult ... place."

Walt stared hard at him. "The adult place?" he repeated. He turned towards Yumiko. "Yumi-chan?"

She smiled sweetly, "Hmm?"

"Just... what is it you're looking for?"

"Just some snack food to take back home."

"Oh," he said. He looked at the box boy. The boy kept his gaze down.

Will turned back to Yumiko. "And, what was it you asked for help in finding just now?"

"Oh, just some penis butter."

Will stopped. He looked at the boy who turned almost purple, but shrugged his shoulders and glanced at Will with a kind of "I told you so" look.

Yumiko continued, "I told Tomoko I would bring her back a large bottle of penis butter. But I can't remember if she wanted smooth or crunchy."

The boy and Will looked at one another. "Peanut butter!! You're looking for peanut butter. Pea <u>nut</u> butter."

"That's what I said."

The boy looked relieved.

"You weren't saying it right, honey. It's pea-<u>nut</u> butter."

"But surely it takes more than just one peanut to make a whole jar, doesn't it?"

Will looked at the stock clerk, who quickly turned to busy himself with fixing items on a shelf. Clearing his throat he said in an extra polite voice, "That... would be... aisle seven." He turned and left in a hurry.

That was one of many incidents which made Will wonder just how good the English was that was being taught in Japan, where Yumiko had her own English school.

The wedding went off without too many hitches. Most of the Japanese guests remembered to leave their shoes on when they walked into the house, but couldn't help bowing from time to time. When a handshake was offered, they gladly accepted. All except Akihiro-san, who wore his finest kimono, and bowed deeply when Walt offered him his hand. Walt, unbowed, pretended to get a hand and proceeded to shake his hand in the air. There they were, one bowing, the other shaking an imaginary hand. They disliked one another instantly.

The reception was held at the Ramona Estates Clubhouse, where a cake was served and lots of drinking and singing went on. Ayla Michaela tried on a beautiful gift yukata, and attempted a Japanese folk dance. Will tried to sing "Sakura", and Yumiko and Will sang "Que Sera, Sera" as a duet. The Japanese guests tended to stay together to talk with one another, while Will's friends tended to talk with other English speakers.

The next day the Japanese guests got up early and played golf. Then they left for Las Vegas and the Grand Canyon.

Yumiko and Will went to Catalina Island for a brief honeymoon. A week later they were in Japan, planning the Gotemba-Kogen reception.

Nakamura Gakuen

Since Yumiko owned her own English school, and it would take at least a couple of years or so to get her students and the schools she serviced used to the idea that she would eventually leave to live in the U.S., it was decided that Will would give up his teaching job in Long Beach, and work at an English immersion school in Numazu to which he had applied and been accepted while on the earlier trip to meet Yumiko's family.

The school he was to work at was Nakamura Gakuen, one of the first true immersion schools in Japan. He would be teaching third grade Japanese students mostly Math, and a little Social Studies and PE.

Yumiko bought Will a train pass and rode with him the first time. This was a commute he would make daily, counting the stops at first—until his ear got used to hearing the names of the stations that were called out. The counting technique almost got him into trouble when a new stop, Nagaizumi Nameri was added.

Once Will got off the train at Nagaizumi Nameri to explore. The newly paved sidewalks contained arrays of lights that shot upwards into the air. Small statues stood around the flat areas adjacent to the beautifully constructed station.

After they got to know one another, Tsukamoto-sensei, (a teacher and one of Will's Third Grade partners who also lived in Gotemba), and Will often rode the train to work together. Will read the Asahi Shimbun in English, while Tsukamoto read his Japanese version. There were many students from various schools on the train, all wearing their sailor suit school uniforms with matching backpacks.

The children chatted noisily, while older passengers tended to keep to themselves. Always there were those who tried to get in an extra few winks of sleep. The train was almost always on time, unless a typhoon had made the tracks impassable. Sometimes there were as many as twenty people on one train car using their keitai (mobile phones) to play games, or to call a parent or flirt with a friend, in spite of posted signs asking that they not be used.

Occasionally when coming home Will would see a high school student spread out on a seat, his book bag taking up part of it and his feet propped up on the seat ahead of him. An old man or woman might be standing nearby, carrying a bag of groceries in one arm and holding on with their other hand as best they could, with nowhere to sit. Often Will gave up his own seat.

These high school students reminded Will of American high school students—all trying to make an impression on one another. The girls would look normal when they first got out of their mother's car in the morning and headed up the steps of the Hakone entrance to the Gotemba eki (train station). By the time their mothers had driven away and the girls had crossed the covered bridge going across the tracks and were headed down the steps to the train platform, their skirts had somehow magically risen to about eight inches above their knees or more. The boys, on the other hand, seemed to think it was sexy to wear their pants as low as possible—far below the normal belt line until Will wondered how they didn't trip over their pant legs. Many of them dyed their hair—blonde or even red. "Ah, youth," thought Will.

Sometimes on Friday afternoons, Tsukamoto-sensei and Will would walk the extra distance to the downtown Numazu eki (train station) for the trip back to Gotemba. There they would grab a beer and bag of senbei and settle into a comfortable seat on the Asagiri express. The smooth-riding, modern looking train sat up higher and stopped only once before reaching Gotemba. There were electric messages in Japanese and English, as well as a recorded woman's voice that made announcements along the way. Will noted, thankfully, that the tones were smooth and professional, and not the baby-talk used by the office secretary at Nakamura Gakuen when she made announcements.

Most of the time, however, they traveled on the older commuter train that went from Gotemba to Minami-Gotemba to Fujioka to Iwanami to Shimo-Togari to Nagaizumi Nameri to Ooka on the way to work.

"Ooka (pronounced Oh Oh kah) desu," came a voice over the speaker. Will realized it was the sixth, uh, seventh stop (later he noticed that the train crossed a wide tributary of the Kanagawa just before reaching Ooka—which would be a good clue for getting his back pack together for exiting the train). It always seemed like half the train got off at the Ooka station, mostly students spilling out the doors and flowing down the sloping walkway.

As Will was passing down the slope and through the turnstile, a cross tone of voice stopped him. An older, uniformed ticket man sat at a window glowering at him. Will felt for his wallet and produced his monthly train pass. "sumimasen, sumimasen," he said. The ticket man waved him through with an irritated gesture, muttering something about gaijin to himself.

Sometimes Will and Tsukamoto-sensei would hitch a ride on the red and white kindergarten bus going to the school, and other times they elected to walk. Walking took about 15 to 20 minutes, but they would sometimes look around at some of the new houses being built or stop off at one of the ever-present Seven/Eleven Stores to pick up a snack (or lunch if Yumiko had not gotten around to making Will's bento).

Always the longest stop was to watch the 20 inch long gray koi swimming lazily in water so shallow their dorsal fins were always exposed to the air. A sign told people the carp were protected, and not to harm or eat them. Will always wondered how they faired when it rained and the water rushed through the shallow cement ditch in a torrent.

Nearing the school, they would see the principal standing out front greeting children, faculty, and parents dropping students off. From the high school next door he could hear high school girls, with their repeated chants of "'zaimasu, 'zaimasu" (short for 'ohayo gozaimasu' or 'good morning'). They reminded him more of the constant lowing of cattle.

The buildings of Nakamura Gakuen (school) were modern, designed by an award winning architect. Will would enter, find his locker, and trade his walking shoes for his indoor Rockport loafers. The Japanese teachers often wore nice suits and ties to work, changing into sweats and workout clothes once inside.

Whenever Will encountered office staff or faculty, they smiled and said, "ohayo gozaimasu" (Good morning). All except Clyde Hasse. Walt had met Clyde at the first faculty meeting. He was new that semester also, (foreign staff tended to turn over fairly quickly—the average duration of employment being two years). One of the few Americans on the staff besides Walt, Dr. Chenoweth and a tall lanky young teacher from New York named Chauncy, Clyde enjoyed coming up with a different variation of "ohayo gozaimasu" every morning-- ".....Ohio gozai-yourself ....Idaho gozaimasu......Columbus gozaimasu.....Iowa gozaimasu.....Arizona gozaimasu......"

Will would "hanko in", (using a Kanji stamp of his name, "Will", creatively designed by Yumiko—with the additional meaning of "one who protects beauty") in the faculty attendance book, then proceed to his computer where he would check his email. There was always a message from the principal, translated by the resident translator for the Immersion Department. "Thank you for fine efforts. There will be visitors from Osaka today. 2I (second grade immersion) and 2R (second grade regular) will go on a field trip today to see the town sewage system. There have been reports of strangers trying to talk with children. Please warn children to be careful." The private elementary school had about 550 students, slightly more than 300 of which were in the immersion program (most of their classes were taught in English), the other half taught mostly in Japanese like a regular school.

Students played on the grounds outside, in a large meeting room inside, up and down the halls, and in unsupervised classrooms in the mornings before school began. "We want them to feel at home," Will was told.

This was one of many differences Will noticed between Japanese and American schools. Another difference was physical contact with students. In America if a student hugs a teacher the teachers are taught to give a quick hug and then walk away so as to not create the suspicion they are trying to become intimate with them. In Japan Will would often see Japanese teachers playing outside with students during recess, and Clyde Hasse would walk around holding two kindergarteners in his arms at the same time.

Americans have succumbed to the appearance of decency at the expense of human touch. It is hard to say if belaying suspicion is worth the cost, especially when so few American students get the attention they need at home. American children are not only separated from others by television, movies and games, they are deprived of therapeutic touching because of overly-cautious school systems and over-worked, under-available parents.

Will's very first day of work was the day after the wedding reception. It was a student free day. The principal picked Will up in his four wheel drive near the Gotemba bus station at 6:00 AM. They drove 3 1/2 hours up to Camp Yatsugatake where the third and fourth grade classes would be going in a few weeks or so. It was called a pre-trip, and it was done every year before each field trip or outing to check out the environment. Will's third grade partners were also in the car, Tsukamoto Akira-sensei, his Japanese partner who spoke very little English, and Cath, a lass from Australia who had taught aboriginal children before coming to Japan. She taught English and Science.

Tsukamoto-sensei was in his early 60's and, like Yumiko and Will, also lived in Gotemba. He came striding up to the meeting place, wearing a dapper, powder blue fishing hat with the brim turned up and a neatly trimmed, white beard, his body tan and lithe from walking long distances whenever he had the chance. Tsukamoto-sensei was an endless source of surprises, and one of Will's favorite people he met while in Japan.

Once, Tsukamoto-sensei invited Will to join him at a kendo match. He never mentioned that he was chairman of the Shizuoka chapter of kendo, or that Will would be placed at his side at a large table while he presided over the event. He was also on the board of directors for a Shinto shrine, and sometimes in charge of the Gotemba matsuri (festival).

Every morning Tsukamoto Akira would honor his parents and grandparents with food at a small altar in his family's classic old ryokan, as well as honoring Mt. Fuji looming out the window. Yumiko and Will were at the ryokan when drunken celebrants came by carrying a small mikoshi (or float). Naturally, Tsukamoto-sensei and his wife plied them with even more sake. Yet another time, Will sat in the dim foyer of his ryokan with several Gotemba elders as a man dressed as a lion came in and danced, and pretended to bite the back of everyone's necks in order to bring them good luck in the new year. Will had to make an impromptu speech at a dinner of some service organization to which Tsukamoto-sensei belonged—and Tsukamoto-sensei was the private guide once when they climbed Fujisan to see an August sunrise.

As the principal had picked them up around six o'clock, it was nine or so in the morning when they passed through a delightful little town called Kiyosato. It had buildings with steep roofs and a quaint little train station. It reminded Will of a village in the Swiss Alps.

That same day had the teachers and principal trudging for miles up and down a mountain trail, then going through an obstacle course, learning the correct way to make bunk beds, checking the classrooms, gym, cafeteria, and observatory—then heading on yet another hike to a spot where they got delicious ice cream cones. The teachers covered most of the activities the students would do over three days in just one, driving back the same night. At one point, hot and tired, they peeled off some layers down to their tee shirts. Tsukamoto-sensei's tee shirt said, "Keep Truckin.'" the principal had an American flag on his, which quoted Kennedy's, "Ask not what your country can do for you, but what you can do for your country." Will had on a black tee shirt with Japanese kanji which said, "kokoro" (heart).

First Day

In Japan the school year starts in April and ends in March. Will was coming in mid-year just after the summer break. There were three major breaks during the year (summer, winter, and near the end of March between school years). There were opening and closing ceremonies at the beginning and end of each break, as well as the beginning and ending of camping, Sports Day, Bazaar Day, and other activities.

During that first Opening Ceremony, Clyde Hasse and Will were introduced to the student body that was lined up in rows outside the school, according to class. They were presented scrolls (by the principal, extending them out with both hands), and identification cards to wear around their necks, and expected to make speeches. Afterwards came a traditional water fight with squirt guns during which everyone became soaking wet.

The children had come prepared with a change of clothes, although Will was a bit taken aback when he saw one youngster totally naked in class while he was changing—unconcerned about the other students.

In class his first day Will took roll. "Kosay --Kousuke---Konousuke -Ryosuke----Ryonousuke-- Yosuke --", (he stopped, and felt his forehead), "...I'm never going to learn these names."

The whole idea behind an immersion school program is to have children learn many of their subjects in a second language, in this case—English. This gives the students a built-in motivation to acquire the new language. Dr. Nakamura, who owned Nakamura Gakuen and several other schools (and lived in a house on the school grounds), had brought in Dr. Chenoweth from Maryland, to head up the immersion school. He, in turn, had gathered credentialed teachers from England, the U.S., Canada, Australia and New Zealand to form the English contingent. They were partnered with Japanese teachers who taught Kanji and other Japanese-related subjects. Now in his seventies, Dr. Nakamura could often be seen in the mornings dressed in a dark suit, taking brisk walks around the school grounds. Rarely was he seen in the Jaguar or the Mercedes parked at his house, a few meters from the entrance to one of his high schools.

Will threw himself into learning the names of his students, the do's and don'ts of Japanese etiquette, making friends with the other staff members, and learning about the community. Most of the teachers had non-descript apartments supplied by the school, close enough they could ride bicycles to work. Yumiko and Will lived in a five story, five sided (Will referred to it as the Gotemba Pentagon) condominium called the Chateau Gotemba, which Yumiko had owned before they met. That meant Will took the train every day. His commute, counting being dropped off at the station by Yumiko, a half-hour train ride, and a walk to school, took just under an hour one way.

Will occasionally went to the barbecues and parties of the other teachers, but had another social life away from the school that involved the Gotemba neighbors and Yumiko's family and friends. Many of their close neighbors at Chateau Gotemba were quite wealthy, coming to the condo in Gotemba as a second residence on weekends and holidays. Most were polite and gracious, and enjoyed bringing them different foods as gifts when they returned from visiting other areas of Japan.

Sadoo

Yumiko's family were often busy with the restaurants, preparing eel or sashimi during the day for the afternoon lunches and dinners. Her brother, Itsuki, did manage to take Will to a baseball game up in Tokyo once. Will was fascinated by the enthusiasm of the crowd. There were regular volunteer cheerleaders who addressed a section of the crowd with bull horns. Itsuki translated one of the cheers as, "Please hit the ball heavenly skyward."

If a batter got a homerun he was presented with a large stuffed toy as he crossed the plate. Instead of a 7th inning stretch, the whole crowd got up after the 8th inning and cleaned the stadium together. Will chuckled at the thought of someone attempting to introduce that custom in America.

Another time Itsuki took Will along to see a sumo match. Although the seats were roped off high up in the seating area, they had been an expensive gift from one of his suppliers.

The wrestlers were enormous and wore skimpy loin cloths. One of them, Itsuki explained, was an American from Hawaii. He looked like a walking mountain as he tossed salt into the ring.

At least once a month the group went to sing karaoke at one of the many clubs or karaoke "boxes."

Yumiko's father, Hirota Akihiro-san, fretted over the loss of the Japanese culture among the youth of Japan. He had a grand collection of chaki, (tea ceremony cups), and loved to preside over tea ceremonies at his own private tea house adjacent to a koi pond, and under a flowering sakura tree, or in the tall grass in the shadow of Mt. Fuji, among other sites. His style was elegant but businesslike, and he clapped his fan and snapped the folds in his fukusa in a macho manner.

Will grew apprehensive at the approach of his first tea ceremony. Luckily, there were only a dozen or so guests attending. They would be served in groups of six, and Yumiko and Will were among the first half dozen. The others watched on from behind.

"Just watch everyone else, and do as they do," Yumiko whispered. "I'll help you through."

The ceremony was being held in a beautiful tea house, open on one side with koi drifting by in a nearby pond. Akihiro-san took great pride in his koi. Three of them he had received as gifts when he was a teenager and were now over two feet in length. He had elegant fish; utsurimo, bekko, kohaku and a beautiful koromo with red outlined in black. They would come to the surface and eat out of his hands. He knew each by name.

"hora Kazuo. kora, kora, Debu-chan, Omaewa iyashiinaa. Chiisai yatsunimo nokoshiteyareyo." ("Here Kazuo. Hey Litle Fatso, now don't be so greedy. Leave some for the little guys.")

The fish even let him scratch their heads. They fell over each other to get to the delicacies he gave them (they especially liked worms and snails).

In the tea room there was a beautiful scroll of kanji (kakejiku) hanging in a tokonoma (alcove), and a tall flower artfully arranged below it.

There was a very thick, long, hollow bamboo pole lying across the middle of the tatami mat floor, with flower blossoms arranged coming up and out of it. Everyone wore kimonos, except for Will who wore his best black funeral suit.

Aka-chan had come with her son, Bisaku, who had immediately gone to take a look at Akihiro-san's zen garden, and then let himself inside the house to look at the Bonkei (tray art) displays. He liked to put his head down even with the models, and imagine himself within the display with the various elements moving all around him. Sometimes he made odd humming sounds as he moved his face in and out.

A young woman assisted Akihiro-san. She had her hair done elegantly, with chopsticks sticking out of it, and a beautiful kimono. She brought water supplies on a tray, setting it down before an unnecessary door, and carefully using her hands three times to slide the door first partly, and then all the way open—bowing to the assembled guests, entering with the tray, and then closing the door in three deliberate motions. She took small, mincing steps without touching the lines separating the tatami mats as she walked, bringing supplies to Akihiro-san.

Akihiro-san sat stiffly on his knees behind a small table/brazier which he used in the ceremony. He had begun preparing hours before the guests arrived, arranging things just so, and folding his fukusa (cloths) carefully before placing them in his obi (sash).

For a few moments he sat in silence. Later Yumiko told Will that Akihiro-san liked to summon up the image of either a brown sparrow sitting on a low branch, or a green tree frog perched half in and half out of a pond before he began. The sparrow observed the correctness of his actions dispassionately as he proceeded and was often there when the atmosphere was more relaxed as with family and friends.   The frog tended to show up for more formal occasions, and tended to be highly critical of the correctness of formalities.   Akihiro's face betrayed no emotion, and he began the long, tedious business of folding his fukusa, wiping off tea containers and bamboo measuring spoons, pre-heating cups with water, etc.

By now Will had been in Japan for several months, and thought he knew a thing or two about Japanese customs. He had even picked up a few words to use at the table while visiting the Hirota restaurants, and was eager to impress people with his new knowledge. Yumiko had told him there were many formalities involved with tea ceremony, but that she would help him out now and then—and he could simply follow what others did.

However, when they arrived Will was seated as the jiyaku (second guest of honor) next to Daisuke Sato-san, a well-known race car driver who, as shokyaku, had the first place of honor while the other four people, including Yumiko, were the kiyaku and tsume, directed to kneel in a line at a right angle to Will and Sato-san. Yumiko would not be close enough to discreetly whisper directions as promised.

"Ai yai yai," said Yumiko, using an expression she'd picked up in California. She looked at Will and shrugged. "Good luck."

Will gave her a doubtful look. "Thanks a lot."

The young woman helping out took small steps over to Sato-san and Will, carrying wagashi, (a tray with what looked like small, gooey green balls covered with powder). She knelt before Sato-san, and bowed to him. Will noticed he had taken a packet of papers out of the folds of his kimono and placed a piece of paper in front of him. The woman then offered the tray. He picked up something that looked like a sharpened twig on the tray, and placed one of the rice dumplings on the piece of paper before him.

The woman then slid the tray over in front of Will. "arigatoo," he smiled, "But, no thanks. I'm on a diet."

The woman didn't move. Will sneaked a look at Yumiko. She was shaking her head in small, quick, shakes. Will reconsidered. Then he remembered he had brought a small packet of Kleenex tissues with him. He pulled them out and placed one in front of him. He then attempted to pick one of the powdered balls up with the stick, but every time he thought he had the little ball balanced, it would plop back down on the dish. Finally, he just picked two of the little buggers up with his fingers and laid them on the tissue.

"ita-daki-masu," he said, pleased he had remembered the phrase one says before eating a meal.

The young woman still didn't move. Everyone was quiet. Will glanced at Yumiko. Her eyes were wide. He realized something was wrong. He counted the mochi-balls. There had been just enough for each person to receive just one. The girl would be going to them with the tray next, and there wouldn't be enough of the little squishers to go around.

"sumimasen. My mistake."

Deep within Akihiro's mind a sparrow began a nervous, periodic chirp.

Walt tried to put one of the mochi tidbits back, but it stuck to the tissue. Then he stripped away most of the tissue and stuck one of the okashi (hideously deformed by this time) back on the tray, licking the sweet white dust from his fingers. Without a blink the young woman proceeded to the others with the tray. Will glanced over at Akihiro-san across the way. He seemed to be deeply concentrating on what he was doing. Perhaps he hadn't noticed anything was wrong. Perhaps.

Will waited for a cue. When Sato-san ate his tidbit, he did the same. "Mmmm. oishii," he said, smiling as politely as he could.

No one replied, but Akihiro-san dropped a bamboo spoon against the side of a cup. Will wasn't sure if that was supposed to happen, or if something had distracted him.

Somewhere a sparrow jumped nervously back and forth from one perch to another.

Akihiro-san took a deep breath. He warmed a chawan (tea bowl) with hot water from the kama and discarded it into a kensui.

Will decided he had better concentrate even harder on the proceedings. Akihiro-san used a piece of bamboo to measure out some green powder into a bowl and added hot water. Then he took what looked like an old-time, bamboo shaving brush and started whisking the tea with it until it got frothy. He seemed to turn the cup around, and handed it to the young woman, who brought it to Sato-san, turned it around again, knelt down and presented it to him. Sato-san picked up the cup, turned it around, and set it down ahead of him and to one side. Then he turned towards Will, put his hands flat together on the mat in front of him, and bowed.

"osakini," he said.

Will studiously copied him, putting his own hands in front of him while facing towards Sato-san and bowed back to him.

"osakini," he said as politely as possible.

Akihiro-san muttered something in spite of himself.

Sato-san seemed disturbed. He bowed and repeated again. a bit more forcefully this time, "osakini."

Yumiko held up a finger to her mouth as "Shhh."

Will held his palms upward. Hadn't he done what the other man had done?

Will's legs were getting tired from the unnatural way he was sitting.

Sato-san turned towards Akihiro-san, and raised his bowl slightly. Then he said, "otemai cho-dai, itashimasu."

Now Will really began to worry. There was no way he would remember all that. There didn't seem to be a lot of tea, but the guy took several (3 ½) sips to get it down—ending with a rather rude slurp and wiping his mouth with his fingers.

By then the young lady had arrived with a steaming bowl of tea for Will. She knelt, bowed, and presented the cup to him. He bowed back to her.

Will bowed again towards Sato-san. "osakini," he said, then turned to wink at Yumiko and see how he was doing. Yumiko did not look back. She was wishing they had never come.

The sparrow squawked and fluttered its wings in alarm.

Now Will desperately tried to remember what the guy next to him had said.

Half-under his breath, he muttered, "moshi ...moshi ..teenie...kini" and then remembered about turning the bowl. He put his hand over it, burning a finger when it accidentally went into the tea. He turned the bowl a bit. It didn't seem to be enough, so he turned it some more. He paused. Then, just to make sure, he turned the whole thing around in a complete circle. Suddenly he remembered something he could say when drinking in public.

Using all the solemnity he could muster he said, "kampai," and downed the hot, bitter green tea in one gulp. He made no rude slurping sounds, and wiped his mouth with the shards of what was left of the tissue. He looked around for some cool water but found none.

Will smiled and gave Akihiro-san an "a-ok" sign with his fingers. With exaggerated gusto he nodded "u—mai", which he figured would please Akihiro-san like it did back at the restaurant. "gotchi so sama deshita."

Yumiko made a little whimpering sound.

Sato-san examined his bowl intently. It had a very irregular shape, and Will felt someone had done a terrible job shellacking it as there were drips down the sides, which had been frozen that way during the kiln process.

Sato-san looked towards Akihiro-san and said, "totemo ii-ocha-wan ii desu ne?"

Will frowned at Yumiko, and raised his eyes upward. He decided he better not let any time go by, so that he might remember something of what Sato-san had said. But it was already too late. He picked up his empty bowl, flipped it over and said, "totem pole obi wan kanobi.... shogun... Disney."

Later he magnanimously offered to help with the dishes, but Akihiro-san was firm in not accepting his offer. It was his first experience with tea ceremony, but not his last. Once again, he learned later he had committed a great many faux pas.

Aka-chan approached Akihiro-san as soon as the ceremony was over.

"Akihiro-san,"("My dear Akihiro-san,") she said. "makotoni mooshiwake gozaimasen." ("Please accept my deepest apologies.")

"hmm?" ("What?") Akihiro-san said, his heart sinking from yet another threat to his event.

"Bisakuga shitewa ikenaikotowo..."("I'm afraid my Bisaku has been meddling where he shouldn't have,") she continued. "moshiwake gozaimasenga, Akihiro-sanga taisetsuni nasatteiru bonkeeo dainashini shiteshimaimashite..." ("I'm afraid he has ruined your Bonkei display.")

Akihiro-san looked up sharply. He had spent many hours on the displays and felt they were a part of him. The only thing worse than them being damaged would have been to discover one of his older koi like Kazuo had passed away.

Akihiro-san raised himself up. He adjusted the crick in his back, sighed, and then headed inside to look at what had happened to his bonkei display.

"hontooni mooshiwake gozaimasen." ("I am so sorry,") Aka-chan said when they reached it. "mattaku nanio kangaete itanoka wakaranakute..., saikin okashina koto shitebakaride...."("I don't know what he must have been thinking. He has been very disturbed lately.")

But Akihiro-san did not notice her chatter. Instead he was looking at the bold, beautifully balanced lines in the Bonkei display. It used most of the same pieces he had used, but orchestrated in a fresh, new, yet somehow still classic way.

"anokoo kokoe." ("Get me the boy,") he said. "kareo saigomade shitemorawaneba."("He must continue with this.")

Aka-chan looked, but Bisaku had disappeared.

The next day Bisaku stuck his head sheepishly inside the door of Hirota's. "oyobidesuka?"("Mom said you wanted to see me.")

Akahiro-san gave him a pad of paper and a pencil. "bonkeino zenkeio dezain dekiruka?" ("Design a bonkei display,") he said.

After that, whenever he was not attending school, jyuku or working with a teacher, Bisaku was busy designing gardens or Bonkei displays. He developed an idea for zen gardens in motion, where the waves of "gravel" became various elements that moved sideways, downwards or upwards. They would sometimes be channeled, and would move outwards and around objects, powered by pumps and gravity. Sometimes water, sometimes floating bits of Styrofoam or colored bubbles.

Bisaku dreamed of building a miniature Mt. Fuji as a hotel in Las Vegas. There would be various samurai processions and historic figures making their way through the casino, which would have quiet contemplative music rather than the loud rockus clanging bells and bright lights of most casinos. There would be a restaurant with waterfalls and koi in walls at eye level to seated patrons, and various forms of his moving Zen gardens along the walls. The idea both fascinated and disgusted Akihiro-san.

Occasionally, on a much smaller scale, Bisaku would actually build something he had imagined. It would be funded by Akahiro-san, who felt mixed emotions about the new tools being used, but liked that the budding young Bisaku had based his creations on age old Japanese tradition.

American Football

Will tried his best to settle into a routine, but found that even riding on the train was an adventure. Many people slept sitting up on the train, regardless of what time of day it was. Sometimes, when it was a bit crowded, he would see a high school student in uniform, leaning against the door of the train with her eyes closed, trying to sleep. He marveled over the faith she had in those doors not opening.

The trains always seemed to run on time (with the exception of when the tracks were flooded during the rainy season). Tsukamoto-sensei told him that the Gotemba line had once had two tracks, but that one set had been torn up to use for war material during WWII.

The train engineers wore white gloves, and referenced items on a checklist with safety signs and landmarks along the way—usually speaking aloud to themselves.

Besides the math and social studies classes he taught to third graders, Will also taught a couple of classes of PE each week.

He tried to do the things the students were used to doing----soccer, Japanese dodge ball, and kickball. However, he had brought along an American football, and decided to give some of the students a "cultural experience."

At first he attempted to explain things on the chalkboard. It didn't seem to be getting through, so he decided to practice a few skills such as passing, catching, and handing off. The class went out to the soccer field, and ran through a few more options. Will's teacher instincts told him he still wasn't being understood. Finally, he decided that learning by doing would be the right solution. They would scrimmage.

Will divided the students into two teams. He selected a center and quarter back for each team, filling in other positions as he went. He demonstrated how to hike the ball. When the students hiked it, the ball usually either went along the ground or over the quarterback's head. The quarterback took the ball, and threw a shovel pass to the center who proceeded to run with the ball, then threw it to another team mate when he thought he was in trouble. That team mate deliberately dropped the ball and began kicking it, soccer style. Immediately all players in the vicinity of the ball, regardless of team, began to kick it as they usually did with a soccer ball. Despite Will's vigorous protests, the ball continued to be kicked until it went into the goal net. Hands went up, "Score!!!"

Will picked up the ball. "Okay," he sighed. "Let's try this again. This time, the other team gets the ball."

He called the center for the other team. "Okay. You saw me show the other center how to hike the ball. I want you to do it exactly the way I showed him how to do it, okay? Exactly. Go."

The center took the ball and walked back to the field. Will directed two of the girls back to their proper positions so they wouldn't be off sides.   When he glanced back, sure enough, the new center was hiking the ball exactly the way he had shown the other center---including the same direction he had been hiking the ball, as well (towards the opposing team).

That's when Will decided the football would make a nice decoration for a corner of his classroom.

In the fall Will was greatly impressed with the athletic prowess the students demonstrated during Sports Day. Most events involved the use of team work.   Third graders had to carry a long stick in groups of 4 in a figure eight course, then come back to where the other students waited. The bar was lowered and each waiting group of four had to jump over the bar.

Will's favorite relay was the first graders whose teams had to carry giant Daruma's made of plaster on a course. The Daruma's (good luck statues) were larger than the little tykes as they ran, dropped the statues, and figured out how to get them back up again.

The event ended with teachers and parents engaged in a giant tug of war with a huge thick rope.

Taiko Wars
(or Thunder on Fuji-san)

Dr. Nakamura had decided that it would be good for the students to have Culture Club once a week. There was a tea ceremony class (simplified for the students), ceramics, shodo (Japanese calligraphy), flower arranging, koto playing, nagauta-bayashi (traditional instruments), and taiko drumming. Teachers went along to help with discipline, but were also allowed to participate in the classes if they paid the same fees as the students. Will wound up with the taiko (drum) club.

"Sagoi," said his friend and teacher-partner, Tsukamoto-sensei. "That means you go to Grand Taiko Tournament at Gotemba Go Gome next week." It turned out that a Go Gome was a fifth –station, one of the traditional starting areas for treks up Mt. Fuji. They are the furthest up which traditional cars are permitted to travel, and command a nice view. There are two or three festivals at the Gotemba Fifth station every year, including a Taiko Competition that draws some of the best competitors from all over Japan, eager to showcase their skills.

Young students and amateur groups bring their own instruments, and are also allowed to participate. More serious competitors appear singly and are allowed to use what some say is the largest taiko drum in the world that must be placed on the wooden stage by crane. The competition stretches over many days, during which the thundering sounds of taiko drums echo down the slopes of the ancient volcano to those below. The thundering ominously foreshadows Fujisan's future.

The Nakamura students had done well the year before and were therefore invited to participate again. They wore traditional happy coats and colorful headbands paid for by their parents. Their taiko teacher came with them, of course—and naturally that meant Will came along, too. Tsukamoto Sensei's Gotemba service group, kind of a combination of the Key Club and the Chamber of Commerce that included the mayor and other city officials, was an integral part of the whole affair.

Posters for the event had gone up six or seven weeks in advance. As an added attraction, Lawrence Melwood the Third, the World's Greatest Gaijin Taiko Drummer would put on a special demonstration of his technique. Will had read an interview with him in the *Daily Yomiuri* in which he waxed eloquently, stressing "...it is in the silences that my full expression resonates with the universal human experience..."

The chartered bus in which the young Nakamura taiko drum performers arrived that morning was air conditioned, thankfully—though the heat and humidity at that elevation was not as oppressive as it had been in Numazu. The group gathered their instruments from the bus's luggage compartment and carried them to picnic tables placed under roofs, which provided shelter from occasional drizzles. Large blue plastic sheets were laid out on which the students sat. Some of the parents had driven up in their fancy cars and kept buying various foods from the surrounding vendors to bring over to the children. The group sat through four or five performances of various groups before it was finally their turn. Will helped to set them up, and soothed nerves with expressions of "Gambatte" and thumbs up. Parents converged on the open air aisles and peppered the performance with ineffective flash bulbs from their cameras.

When a child enters first grade at Nakamura Gakuen he or she is assigned to a "family" that consists of two to four children from each grade. The teachers of the fourth and fifth grade students work with them to create 'programs' that are easy enough for all to do. Roughly once a month the older students arrive at the first grade students' classrooms to pick them up and bring them to another class. While one or two support teachers sit in the back, either doing some of their own work or helping to iron out any thorny problem that might arise, the older students are in charge of running the activity. They provide instruction and encouragement to the younger students in completing whatever the project happens to be. This encourages students to empathize with those who are younger and weaker and less skilled than themselves. It teaches them patience, strengthens leadership skills, and gives them direct positive contact with students with which they might not otherwise interact.

In the schools in Long Beach Will had not seen any similar proactive measures taken. Sometimes kindergartners shared a campus with students up to eighth grade. The only interactions were when older students would deliberately walk through a PE class in which younger students were participating, or steal their lunch money, teach them bad words, or become over-sexed role models leading young students to have far too sophisticated childhoods.

It amazed Will how much countries could learn from one another, and how little they do.

Japanese children often have two or three years of kindergarten. They work all year to create extravagant shows that are well supported by the community---not only by parents but by actively engaged citizens from store owners to mayors of towns. The shows demonstrate important dexterity skills the students have learned (such as tumbling, playing musical instruments, and elaborately choreographed dances performed entirely on unicycles). The tots perform songs entirely in English, and give full length plays such as *The Sound of Music*. Mentally challenged students are also fully included in performances matched to their skill levels.

Here at an inspiring location on the world's most-photographed mountain, children of all ages got to perform before a large, international audience along with some of the world's greatest musicians.

When it was their turn, the children from Nakamura Gakuen hopped onstage and quickly set up their drums to their performance positions. Will helped as best he could, then took up a position squatting down in front of the first row of audience seats.

For the first number, the teacher stood in front. At an unheard direction, the children raised their drum sticks into the air, spread their feet and froze in position. An unworldly sound that pricked the hair on the back of Will's neck came out of the teacher's mouth. Down came the sticks with the precision of a machine. The children played in perfect unison, beating their drums, synchronized perfectly even when raising their sticks into the air at exactly the same time during a rest in the playing. The tempo increased and the volume rose. Students gyrated and their hair flew despite their headbands. With no direction from the teacher, the volume suddenly diminished to a light tapping, then, just as mysteriously, found it's way back to high volume. The students stopped together, spun around, and took up where they had left off. The sound grew louder and louder, and, with no apparent sign of any kind, abruptly ended.

The teacher mounted the stage and stood behind the children for the next piece, playing a shamisen and punctuating pauses now and then with esoteric vocal noises ala nagauta bayashi. Flash cameras, the flashes to no avail at that distance, shot off. The parents went wild cheering for their proud children when they finished.

Will helped remove the instruments and to get them loaded back on the bus. Everyone waited patiently for several other groups to perform. Then there was silence for 10 or 15 minutes or so, while the judges judged and a crane began to set up a giant taiko drum mid-stage. There were several tense moments, while a few honorable mention awards were given, but finally it was announced that Nakamura had placed third over all the schools in their category. That was good enough for all of them to be summoned to the stage to receive a special award presented with two hands by the mayor himself, and the taiko teacher to receive a small plaque and a large bouquet. Several photo sessions later, the teacher and about half the students climbed back aboard the bus to return home, while the rest of the students joined their parents to either leave by car or enjoy more of the competition.

Will decided to stick around to see how good the main competitors really were. He strolled about the booths and tried out various foods, and even sampled some Asahi black beer. Yumiko had told him she would get together with her sister and Atsuko after her clay doll class, and try to meet him sometime in the late afternoon.

It took 30 or 40 minutes to finish setting up the giant taiko drum.

Will was enjoying a second Asahi black when the first contestant strolled out onto the stage. He seemed to be wearing something like a loin cloth, and an abbreviated, sleeveless shirt revealing muscular arms, completely open in front and cut high in back. He strode up the steps of the wooden platform, and stood looking at the drum. After several seconds he raised a drum stick high into the air, and froze in position—one leg stretched forward, the other behind. Then he seemed to lunge towards the drum, giving it a loud thump. He paused, then began rapidly beating it quietly. He beat faster and faster, louder and louder—then suddenly grew very soft---then loud once again.

When he finished the audience applauded enthusiastically. He bowed deeply, and walked briskly down the steps and off the platform.

Several other contestants followed, wearing various interesting costumes which usually revealed muscular arms and legs. Some varied the drumming with loud and soft beats, others attacked the giant drum with a flurry of beats and interesting twirls of the drum sticks. All had their own, individual style—and the enthusiasm of the audience seemed to build with each participant.

The afternoon wore on, and Yumiko and company had not shown up yet. Neither had Lawrence Melwood III, the World's Greatest Gaijin Taiko Drummer, whom Will was curious to see.

Will discovered another booth over towards the parking area which was distributing free samples of shoshu, along with a sweet, carbonated plum drink. He had just downed his second sample, when Tsukamoto sensei came from around a large truck in the parking area, a worried look on his face.

Will waved to him and lifted a glass. Akira Tsukamoto-sensei managed a smile, but hurried on to an officials' tent where he engaged in a spirited conversation with some of the other Gotemba elders. As they spoke, more officials wearing suits and organization arm bands joined the conversation which at times became animated.

Suddenly, Tsukamoto turned around and looked directly at Will. He remained that way, staring at Will across the grass for several seconds, then turned and continued talking with the others. A minute more and he turned again to look at Will. This time, the others turned as well. Will wondered if he had done something wrong again.

Then Tsukamoto walked towards Will in a purposeful way. He was flanked on either side by officials, one who kept wiping his face as they walked.

"Mast-san, ogenki desuka?" he said.

"Genki desu," Will replied, smiling pleasantly at his friend and his companions and wondering why the pleasantries when there was something obviously of a pressing nature on his mind.

"I hope you enjoy," he said, using more English than Will had recalled him using in the past.

"Yes, Tsukamoto-sensei—very much so." The man next to Tsukamoto continued to sweat profusely—

looking dubiously at Will, sizing him up and down. "Is there anything I can do for you?"

"Maybe. Maybe so, Will-san," he said, and his eyes appeared to be begging.

Whenever Tsukamoto-sensei said 'maybe' to Will, he had learned that he really meant 'definitely'. 'Maybe' was simply a form of politeness, meant to soften a request.

"Well, what is it? I'll be glad to help if I can."

Tsukamoto said something to the other men in Japanese. They suddenly seemed relieved and started smiling. "Arigatoo gozaimasu," one said, bowing extremely low. The other man came forward and shook Will's hand. "Thank you. Thank you vely much, Will-san. You fine man. Fine man vely much."

"Will-san," Tsukamoto-sensei continued. "Maybe you come with me?"

Will's apprehensions began to grow. He hadn't the faintest idea what was being asked of him, but he felt as though he was already committed somehow.

The two of them made their way through the parking lot to a large camper. There Tsukamoto-sensei knocked on the door. Immediately it opened, and another official wearing an arm band on his suit looked at Will with terror.

Tsukamoto said something to the official, who gave a doubtful look at Will before stepping aside.

"dozo," said Tsukamoto-sensei, practically pulling Will inside.

Will entered and his eyes adjusted to the light.

At the far end was a small, pale, wiry looking man sitting on the camper's bed.

The little man shakily rose to his legs. "Lawrence Melwood the Third," he announced in a strong English accent. He started to hold out his hand, then lunged for a sink and threw up.

Lawrence Melwood the Third was tanked to the gills.

Hear My Thunder

"kichi gai. Not in a million years," Will said.

"You must," pleaded Tsukamoto-sensei. "I told already that you help."

"But I didn't know you needed that kind of help."

"You playing with class many weeks now..."

"Once or twice. On <u>little</u> drums. I never even saw a drum that big until a couple hours ago. Besides", Walt said, looking at Melwood, "we don't look anything alike."

"You both gaijin. No one know." The little man was now swaying as he looked back and forth at the speakers with great interest. He was pale, scrawny, and probably stood about 5 foot 4 inches, and was beginning to bald. Walt was a couple inches shy of six feet and 180 lbs., with a full head of hair beginning to gray.

"How anyone could take me for him I'd never know."

Melwood raised a finger. "The secret," he confided, "is in the silences…" His eyes rolled back in his head as he passed out cold.

Tsukamoto quickly pulled Will back outside, and took him around the corner of the camper. "I not ask this if not very much desperate. People come long way to see Melwood-san."

He looked at Will in the eyes, foreigner style. "This is the good mayor. He good for Gotemba. He disgraced if no Merood-san. He have to resign, and some staff resign also."

Will knew he would regret his decision, either way. He saw the pleading look in his friends face, the desperation of a man with no choices. Perhaps he could be brave for his friend, or perhaps he'd had just the right combination of beer and shochu. He held up his hands. "I don't have anything to wear."

x x x x x x x x x x x x x x x x x x x x x x x

The audience was beginning to stir. Three acts had already gone on after the announcement had been made that the great Melwood-san would appear later in the program.

"What the hell am I doing this time?" thought Will. "What besides a little beer and shochu had made me dream I could ever pull this off?"

Now he was wearing almost skin tight pants borrowed from another contestant, no shirt, half an ounce of sun tan oil and had a bandana tied tightly around his head. Someone had put thick hair oil on his hair, and pulled it into tufts going in all directions (a touch that perplexed Will, but to which he didn't complain). As he strode towards the stage he grabbed some wrap around sunglasses that belonged to a stage hand and slipped them on without breaking stride.

Will could hear the restlessness in the audience, and then a sudden hush as he walked onto the stage. There was no announcement in Japanese, either because they felt none was needed, or because the announcer couldn't bring himself to tell the public lie of which they were all conspiring. The small crowd of that morning had now swelled to several hundred people, waiting in anticipation. They were people who were brought up on taiko, listened to taiko recordings, discussed the strengths and weaknesses of various taiko artists.... people who would probably see through Will before he ever even touched the drum.

Will continued to stride boldly across the stage, and bounded lightly up the steps to the drum. Then, he turned to the audience that felt like an immense beast about to consume him, and bowed deeply.

Then he turned back towards the drum.

It was enormous. It had looked big from the audience, but from close up it was gargantuan. All he could do was stare at it. He could see the various discolorations on the head where it had been beaten the most, and remembered that different tones seemed to have been gotten out of different locations on the smaller drums he had used.

He continued to stare for what felt to be an eternity. The audience remained in rapt silence. There wasn't even a cough.

"This is it," Will thought. "This is where I become the laughing stock for several hundred people. I'll probably have my visa revoked."

He thought about the most dramatic poses he had seen earlier that day. Suddenly, he raised his arms above his head, put one foot forward, the other far back. Then he arched his back as far as he could until he looked directly up to where the top of Fujisan was hidden in a cloud.

He brought his arm back....and froze. At that moment, he was seized with a tremendous, paralyzing fear.

"It's now or never," he thought---and wheeled his arm forward with all his might. Wham! It struck solidly, and the sound reverberated through the admiring crowd and down the slope of Fujisan.

He stayed in that position for a joyous full second. For a joyous, full second, he <u>was</u> Lawrence Melwood the Third, the Great Gaijin Taiko Drummer.

He wanted to play. He wanted to beat that giant taiko as hard and fast as he could. He wanted to beat fast and furiously, then slow and quietly. He wanted the crowd to listen, and to appreciate, and enjoy. He wanted to tease them and to play with their emotions. He wanted the sounds to reverberate down the slopes from Gotemba Go-chome into the city below. He wanted to become one with the sound. He knew the audience was with him, and he felt the power he held at that moment as the audience waited for what was to come next.

And then he did...........................nothing. Then ...... even more....nothing.

Then he stopped and stood away. He bowed to the hulking drum. He bowed to the audience, turned, and began to walk off the stage. From the corner of his eye he could see people in the front rows sitting with bewildered looks on their faces. He continued to walk, the suddenly very, very long way back, very long and very, very quiet.

Someone near the back of the audience who was either sadistic, dangerously insane, or had a sick sense of humor began to clap. He or she, was all alone for several seconds. Then another, closer to the stage, joined in clapping. The two of them clapped together— as though unafraid of what the rest of the audience thought. A man shook his head in admiration, the way Will once saw a Parisian marvel at an existentialist walking backwards around a chalk circle he had scrawled on a sidewalk. Then there was another clapper---and suddenly the whole crowd erupted in waves of applause followed by cheering.

As he neared the edge of the stage, a photographer snapped Will's picture. A woman ran up to him with a program and a pen.

Will took the pen and signed, "L. M. III" with a great flourish.

"arigatoo gozaimasu," she said with deep admiration.

Will handed the program and pen back to her. "The secret," he said, "is in the silences."

The woman didn't understand a word he said, but she blushed excitedly and nodded as if she did and looked at the signature as a treasure.

A few more people came up with programs, which he also signed. He felt another one touch his back, and turned to find Yumiko and her sister, Sanae, holding up programs for him to sign. They both gasped when they recognized him.

Will held up a finger to his lips. "Shhhh," he begged. Then, looking around, "The secret is ...is in silence."

He gave them a knowing look. Then quickly under his breath, "And besides, Tsukamoto-sensei and the mayor would have lost face." Will left the thoroughly baffled women, walked back out for another bow, then off the stage and back to the trailer.

Will thought he had actually pulled it off. The next day one of his students caught him off guard when he remarked how much he looked like Lawrence "Merood" the Third.

Gotemba Matsuri

Some nights Will would get off the train and go directly to Hirota's to wait for Yumiko to finish teaching her English classes. They would often go to 8:00 PM or later. Chauncy, one of the Nakamura teachers, had come along one hot August night, to "chew the fat" awhile. School was not in session, but Will had been tying up some odds and ends that day and had met Chauncy as he left, jogging along the road.

Chauncy was very tall and thin with short blond hair (sometimes shaved completely) and wielded a sarcastic wit. He had a photographic memory when he wanted to. He studiously wore his sweatshirt inside out, and had two pairs of sandals exactly the same at school, so that no one could tell if he had changed his shoes or not when he entered. His Japanese was far better than Will's, Will's being practically non-existent, and he was committed to the Zen of jogging around town, often without a shirt, (even though he had been stopped numerous times by city police officers and told to go home and put one on).

The two teachers trudged up the steps and made their way back along the second floor patio area past the Zen garden towards Hirota's entrance. Will had helped to build the Zen rock garden along with Fukumoto, George, and Yumiko's brother, Itsuki. There were long lines of raked gravel that swept around reddish volcanic rocks and a miniature Fujisan, also created with gravel. Bamboo screens hung behind. A long, narrow table stood across from the two noren-draped doorways. There were several vases, tea ladles, potted hydrangeas, and bottles of shochu and sake lined up on the table—and a sign telling of that evening's specials. Near one door was a small kind of water-zen garden designed by Bisaku that utilized a water pump and a corrugated piece of plastic to guide streams of water down and around bits of moss-covered rock and pieces of wood, and a small bonsai in a hollowed piece of volcanic rock. By the other door was a traditional statue of a raccoon dog, proudly displaying his oversized genitals to incoming patrons.

"irrashaimase", was always the greeting from Akihiro-san.

"Good evening, Will-san," smiled Sanae as she passed by with a tray of food for a back table. Sanae knew about as much English as Will knew Japanese, but she liked to use it when she saw him.

"kon bon wa," ("Good evening") the teachers chorused. Will introduced Chauncy.

Upon entering one found another small table, featuring a keg of sake to be opened and shared with all present if the Giants or Swallows won the championship, and copies of two of Yumiko's books she wrote on how to learn English which were on sale, complete with CD's inside the jackets for practicing. Inside the restaurant was the glass counter behind which Akihiro stood, wearing his ever-present bandana and preparing the various dishes.

Often Will sat on a stool in front of the glass counter—sometimes watching the TV or looking at the autographs of baseball players or Richard Gere who had eaten there once while making an Akira Kurasawa film. Akihiro had pictures of Yakult Swallow baseball players, as well as Giants. Of course, there were also Ichiro (who was the first Japanese position player to go to the US) and Matsui, (known as "Godzilla" who was still with the Yomiuri Giants at that time but would later become the most valuable player in the 2009 World Series playing for the New York Yankees).

In the center of the room was a square counter area described earlier that was surrounded with low stools, inside of which was a non-functional irori, with a cooking pot above which was a large metal fish. The 'fire' below the pot was made with red chili peppers. On the walls were hung an old-style straw raincoat, hat, and boots, and a wooden kendo sword. There were platforms at one end, separated by paper walls, on which were tatami mats. Guests would sit there cross-legged to eat at low tables. Through a door was a bathroom with a traditional Japanese toilet that looked to Will more like a urinal set on the ground. A cash register was on the other side of the front door, with Hirota business cards featuring a picture of an eel. Next was a glass case with beer and shochu mixes, followed by the namae beer machine (tap), and a long narrow corridor running along the kitchen to another part of the restaurant, where there was yet another entrance, Japanese toilet, and tatami rooms which could be made larger or smaller by the placement of sliding paper walls.

Chauncy and Will chose a couple of stools around the center square area and away from the door, and ordered nama beer from Sanae-san. "kampai," they toasted. Akio-san, the gentleman farmer and fisherman who had been a friend of the family for as long as Yumiko had known, raised his glass from one end of the other counter. They saluted him back.

Sanae brought them complimentary shirasu (a bowl full of miniscule white fish with small, beady black eyes), one of the benefits of being family. Shirasu was not Will's favorite, but he knew Akihiro-san had probably already thrown some yakitori on the grill—and it was some of the best he'd ever had in Japan.

One sometimes thought twice before spending an evening with Chauncy. He was a font of knowledge when it came to books on Japan, Japanese history, and many cultural pursuits. But, he would also come out with abrupt statements about his host country that were none too flattering....usually at inopportune moments. Things like "When adjusted for total numbers of prisoners taken during WWII, American prisoners taken by Germany had ten times more chance of surviving the war than did prisoners taken by Japan."

He was hopelessly lost in a love/hate relationship with Japan, which some said spilled over into his relationship with his Japanese wife as well.

The teachers quaffed their beers, and put togarashi on their yakitori when it arrived. Will ordered a plate of sashimi, and some musamushi (a kind of egg pudding with bits of vegetable and eel inside), while Chauncy ordered salted sama fish.

Chauncy was the only New Yorker Will had ever met who liked to surf. They spent a lot of time comparing breaks they had found, but both agreed there wasn't anything worthwhile within an hour's drive of Numazu or Gotemba. Most of what they saw at places like Shimoda or the beaches near Kamakura had the surf culture, but not any good surfing. There were surf shops in all these places, and one could trade surf stories with other foreigners at the Speakeasy in Numazu, or the mini-brewery place by the docks—but there was more talk than action.

Chauncy had guided Will to many a good book on Japan. Will had found <u>Shogun</u>, and <u>Gaijin</u> by James Clavell on his own, but Chauncy had turned him on to a book written by Musashi, Japan's foremost swordsman, to paintings by Musashi, to <u>Ryoma, A Renaissance Samurai,</u> to <u>Ranald MacDonald, Native American in the Land of the Shogun,</u> <u>Lost Japan,</u> <u>You Gotta Have Wah</u>, (about major league baseball players in Japan), <u>How to Bow,</u> <u>The Last Shogun,</u> <u>Dave Barry Does Japan,</u> <u>Kokoro </u>(Lefcadio Hearn), and the writings of Basho.

He was just telling Will how he had traveled part of Basho's northern route once, visiting places like Yamadera, when a young man entered and took a seat near the other end of the four sided center counter area.

"irrashaimase," hollered Akihiro-san.

"irrashaimase," said Sanae-san.

"kon ban wa," greeted the man. "nama biru, kudasai." ("Draft beer, please.")

"hai."

"masta…"

"hai."

"unagi, onegashimasu."

"hai, domo."

Unagi is Japanese for eel, which is Hirota's specialty. It is considered good for one's health to eat eel when the weather is hot. Yumiko and Will usually would help out on National Eel Eating Day (in August) because Hirota's would always be packed with people from morning to night, plus having to deliver to Pachinko Parlors or community meetings. The eel is often served in an unaju, a rectangular lacquered box on a bed of rice, with sauce and seasonings. It was often accompanied with cucumbers and eel heart soup.

When the man turned back he seemed to notice the two Americans for the first time, and gave a sour look away. The look was not lost on Chauncy.

"What have we here?" muttered Chauncy not really under his breath. "As the press tells us, there's certainly no anti-foreigner sentiment left in this country."

The young man's eyes narrowed. Will could tell he had begun his drinking earlier in the evening. "I know what you are saying."

"Another product of the Japanese education system, no doubt," rejoined Chauncy, "which means you know next to nothing about your country's modern history."

"I know enough about history to say that Americans should watch what they say this month."

"You mean about Gotemba's matsuri day?" They had begun to hear occasional fireworks outside.

"I mean when your President Truman ordered the bomb dropped on women and children," he said, his voice growing threatening.

Akihiro-san looked up abruptly from his work, noticing the tone of voice. His work slowed as he watched.

There was a smile on Chauncy's face as he warmed to the attack. "You think he should have been a traitor to his own people? You think he should have ordered a D-Day type landing instead, killing, oh, some

300 thousand or more Americans and even more Japanese?"

"There's no reason the bombs couldn't have been dropped on unpopulated areas," the young man said pointing his finger, "instead of on innocent women and children."

"None except that it could have easily been denied by the same Japanese generals who tried to continue the war even after the emperor said it was over—the ones who were getting those women and children you talk about to sharpen bamboo poles for fending off the machine guns and tanks that would have come in a landing."

The man switched to Japanese at that point.

The young man said, "jikanno mudadana. nani ittatte, omaetachi amerikajinwa zettaini sensono hio mitomenaindakara!" ("Why do I waste my time? You Americans will never admit your stupid crimes, never!")

To which, Chauncy replied in fluent Japanese; "amerikawa jibuntachino okashita ayamachio mitomeru, yuiitsuno kunidesu. amerikano kodomotachiwa senjuuindeanga donna atsukaio uketakamo, 150 nenmaeno kokujindoree-mondaino kotomo, gakkoode benkyooshite, shitteimasu. kyookashonimo kaite arimasukara." ("America is the only country honest enough to admit its crimes. Every school child in America knows how the Native Americans were treated, and about the slavery issue of 150 years ago—it's in our school books.") "jissai, nihonno kodomodesaemo, sono kotoo shitteimasu. Demo, ittai nanninno nihonjinno kodomoga, jibunno kuniga, takadaka 7,80 nenmaeni chuugokuya kankokude shita kotoo shitteirundeshooka? Sonokotoga notteiru kyokasho o mitemitai desu ne." ("In fact, even Japanese school students know about it. But how many Japanese children know what <u>their</u> country did in China and Korea just 70 or 80 years ago? Show me that in a Japanese text book.") "kekkyokuwane, wakai nihonjinno hotondowa, shinjuwan-koogekino kotoo kiita kotomo naindesuyo." ("Hell, most young Japanese never heard of Pearl Harbor.")

The young man put down his chopsticks. He stood up: "Omaetachiwana, misekakeno kirisutokyoono rinenni kakureta, gizennteki-shyuukyoo-suuhaishadana. bakabakashii!" ("You pretend to be so pious, hiding behind your hypocritical Christian morality. Stupid!")

Chauncy stood up. Akihiro-san hurriedly wiped his hands and began to come around the counter to get his kendo sword.

Chauncy: "daremo watashiga kirisutokyoo-shinjanadoto iimasen. awatete machigatta ketsuronni tadoritsukimashitane. nihonni ite ichiban ii kotowa, shinkarono hiteesuru seishono kageki-enzetsushao mikakenai kotodesu." ("Nobody calls me a Christian. You have jumped to conclusions. One of the things I like best about Japan is there aren't a bunch of bible thumpers disputing evolution.") "maa, mochiron, anatawa, shizeno suuhaishite, shigono sekaio yokushiyooto shiteirundeshookedone. dokokarakano, karimonono shyuukyooni narattene." ("Of course, <u>you</u> probably believe in worshipping nature and then improving your after-life odds by adhering to a borrowed religion as well.")

The young man, taking a step to one side: "Omaemo, zuibun tonchinkanna kotoo yuuna. Orewa, konoyode shuuukyoooonante iraneeno." ("You have also jumped to conclusions. I need no spiritual crutches of any kind in this life.")

Suddenly Akihiro-san was there. He stood with his wooden kendo sword, first threatening the young man, then threatening Chauncy.

"nani?" cried Chauncy, his eyes wide in mock disbelief. "ee~? kimiwa shinkooshinga nai hitonanoka?" (What? You are a disbeliever?") Suddenly, he was wheeling about in mock despair, like the Lee Marvin character in the Marlon Brando film *The Wild One*. He grabbed Will by the shirt. "Oh, the shame of it all, Johnny! The shame! What would mother think?"

Akihiro-san looked at him as though he had gone crazy. "Do you mean," he continued, " you face life with no (in Japanese) 'shinkooshin?' ('spiritual crutches'?) To tempt the vastness of eternity with the blasphemous notion that there just ain't nothin' afterwards?!"

He approached the young man. Akihiro-san raised his wooden sword high in a threatening manner.

"I cannot believe I am hearing this," Chauncy clapped his hands over his ears. He continued in a Mercutio-like way. "Nor will I permit these eyes to continue to witness such a sight." He covered his eyes, then his mouth, "I shall not permit these lips to utter such terrible evil."

He wheeled around and grabbed the passing Sanae-san by both arms, and looked into her eyes. "nokosareta hoohoowa, hitotsushika arimasen." ("There is only one choice left for me.") Suddenly he grabbed the wooden kendo sword from Akihiro-san. "sepuku!"

He thrust the wooden blade between his arm and torso, then pretended to slice open his belly. He then fell full length on his back across a section of the square counter, his head coming to rest in a flower arrangement.

The young man smiled in spite of himself. Akihiro-san angrily grabbed for the kendo sword.

At that moment there was a crash of glass and a divine intervention as a gust of wind came through the newly opened door. A group of drunken revelers poured into the room. They were good Gotemba citizens, young and old, wearing navy blue, turquoise, black, and white happy coats which said Gotemba, and "Hirota's" in stylish kanji, with an outline of Fuji-san on the back. Their head scarves, sashes, and knee leggings were all emblazoned with black eels, head to tail.

Oblivious to the mood of what had been transpiring moments before, the men were doing their best to perform their civic duties—participating fully in the Gotemba matsuri, marching, shouting, and getting as drunk as possible. Several hailed Akihiro-san, who was their sponsor, first bowing then throwing an arm around him. Some made straight for the toilets at either end of the restaurant, and others could be observed whenever the door opened, relieving themselves on the plants outside.

Sanae-san brought out two enormous bottles of sake but Akihiro-san stopped her, and instead opened the large wooden keg of sake meant for the baseball playoffs. A stack of square wooden sake cups were scooped up by the group, and soon there were shouts of "kampai!"

One of the men thrust cups into Chauncy and Will's hands. Chauncy picked up another cup and took it over to the young man. He murmured in Japanese. "sono tokiwa, tadashii kotoo shimashitaga, jinruinitottewa ozomashii dekigotodeshita. – nidoto kurikaeshitewa naranai kotodesu." ("Though it _was_ the right thing to do at the time, it was a horrible event for mankind—and must never happen again.") "nihonwa, hanseeki ijoomono aida, koogekitekini derukotomo naku, hinkon-shokokuni taisuru koukendowa, amerika, chuugoku, kankoku o tashita monoyori ooi n desu. Sooyuu atarashii nihonni kanpai." ("Japan has not been aggressive in more than a half century and contributes more to poor countries than the US, China, and Korea combined. To that new Japan, I drink,") he paused and looked at the young man, "sorekara, misekakeno shuukyooshino motazu, yuukanni shini mukaiau kotoga dekiru hitotachinimo kanpai." ("and to anyone honest and brave enough to face death without hiding in religious lies.") He lifted his cup.

The young man looked at the cup given him, shrugged—raised it up, downed it and smiled.

There was a general sigh of relief, even by some patrons who had studiously pretended not to notice anything earlier.

"To Hirota-san," said Chauncy. "Hirota-san!" the men cheered.

Akihiro-san seemed pleased. "are? Motohiro-santo Tsukamoto-senseito, hokano hitotachiwa, dokoni...?" ("But where are Motohiro, Tsukamoto-sensei, and the others?") he asked.

"mikoshino miharini itteru yo." ("Down guarding the mikoshi,") said Oburo-san, a Nakamura Trustee who lived a block from Hirota's and came in regularly.

"nomisugite, kaidanmo noborenaindaroo." ("Too drunk to climb the stairs,") said a young man, with bleached blond hair.

"Tsukamoto-senseiwa hitoiki tsukini, ieni kaettato omoimasuyo." ("I think Tsukamoto-sensei went home to pass out,") said another.

"jaa, kawariga irudaroo." ("Then you will need replacements,") said Akihiro-san. He took a couple of unagi decorated headbands and thrust them towards Chauncy and Will.

Chauncy tied his around his head immediately. "hai, domo," he said. "This is gonna be great!" he added with relish.

"I've never done this. What do I do?"

"Just do what everyone else does."

A worried look came over Will. "I've heard that before."

Two happy coats came hurtling across the counter at them. "hora," ("Here,") commanded Akihiro-san.

They slipped on the happy coats and started towards the door. Yumiko entered with one hand shielding her eyes. She looked at Chauncy and Will wearing their happy coats and headbands and laughed. Then she grew quickly angry, looking at her father. "otoo-sanno ajisaini oshikkoshiteiru hitoga iruwayo." ("There is a man doing pee on your hydrangea!") she said.

"futarida." ("Two men,") said an old man, swaying dangerously by the door.

"sannin," ("Three,") said another, looking out the door as it opened.

She stared at him. "nante hitotachinano? shigikaini uttaeteyaru." ("What kind of people you are? I am going to write a letter to the city council,") she announced.

The old man looked at her. "oretachiga shigikaiinnandakedo..." ("We ARE the city council.")

"dattara, ima sugu itte yamesasetekudasai!." ("Then tell them to stop peeing on our plants right now!")

Someone slid the door open. There were several men standing with their backs to the door, busily watering the plants.

A man stood near the door, swaying, "ima sugu yamero tte itteruzo." ("She says to stop that right now.")

"ima, ima!" ("Right now!") demanded another emphasizing it by pointing at the floor.

A man farted. Another man looked over his shoulder, and feebly tried to wave off the annoyance. That threw off his aim, and a stream of urine arced over the balcony and splattered on to a man stretched out snoring on the mikoshi below.

Chauncy grabbed Will's arm and yanked him towards the door. "Time to go. shitsurei shimasu." ("Excuse us").

Will caught Yumiko's eye and shrugged, "Hi..... goodbye. Sorry."

She immediately was all smiles. "Don't be sorry. You have good time."

"Thanks, Sweetie."

One of the drunken men, who spoke some English, looked up incredulously, "Sweetie? You call her Sweetie?" Then, as Will and Chauncy walked out the door, he shook his head "Sweetie."

x x x x x x x x x x x x x x x x x x x x x

Outside there were people making their way in all directions, including climbing up and down three sets of stairs which came up to Hirota's from the street level. There was a man seated on a parking curb, and another with his back propped up against a support column. The man who had so rudely been showered on while sleeping on the mikoshi had gotten up and was making his way slowly upstairs. He found the hose outside of Hirota's and washed himself off. It was a warm evening and it wouldn't have hurt anything, except that when he went to turn it off he ended up turning another hose on instead, and left both running before he went back downstairs.

Chauncy, Will and their new companions were gone before the water had covered a considerable portion of the upper patio and began to fall in sheets to the floor below. But not before much time had passed in getting organized. The mikoshi, which in this case was a small float carried on the shoulders of participants, is used in a parade of drummers, musicians, and other revelers as they march around the town. The rest of the parade had long since passed on, but the group could hear the music of the parade several blocks over and figured they could catch up with them.

Getting everyone to just be at the mikoshi at one time took some doing. As soon as one side seemed complete, someone left from the other side to take a leak or to pet a cat, admire the stars, or to go on some conjured up errand. Finally, they all heaved the mikoshi up to their shoulders at the same time. Things looked good for a moment. Then, synchronizing with a chant, they took the first step, almost all at the same time. Unfortunately, they weren't all facing the same direction. The mikoshi lurched sideways and plunged wildly down to the pavement.

Thankfully, Oburo-san came down and took command. A trustee of Nakamura Gakuen and a natural leader it wasn't long before he had everyone chanting, lifting, grunting, and stepping along. It seemed to take forever for them to catch up with the rest of the parade, but finally they slid in between the taiko section and a group of young girls wearing yukatas and elaborate face make up that looked like black question marks painted in the middle of their faces.

The parade made its way down the main street then took a turn towards the train station, passing Tsukamoto's ryokan along the way. Junko, Mrs. Tsukamoto, came out wearing a mustard colored kimono and carrying two enormous bottles of sake. The mikoshi group immediately fell out of the parade, set the mikoshi down and dutifully passed around the sake. Tsukamoto-sensei himself was nowhere to be seen, having been carried home unconscious by concerned citizens and some of his kendo students sometime earlier.

When the contingent moved on the mikoshi was dipping and swaying precariously. A block later they passed a small alleyway. Some of what Chauncy was calling the "mikoshi pall bearers" were mysteriously drawn to the alley. Others were too drunk to resist. Before long, the group had moved sideways like a crab, half-way down the alley before those who realized they were going in a wrong direction managed to stop and get the sideways momentum going back the other way. When they got back to the street, the rest of the parade had gone on without them. They never did catch up after that. Some crawled back to the steps in front of Tsukamoto's ryokan to pass out.

A handsome young black marine from Camp Fuji came down the street with his arm around a beautiful young Mexican hooker with dark flowing hair. They stared at the mikoshi sitting on the side of the road, and the revelers holding their heads or sleeping in bushes or doorways, then made their way to the stairs outside her apartment.

Yumiko found Chauncy and Will and loaded them into the Honda. She tried to get Yasunobu in as well, but every time she got in to drive, he climbed out the other side. Chauncy said it would be dangerous to have him in the car and that he would be just fine where he was until morning. Then he put his head against the back side window and fell asleep.

Fujisan

The official climbing season for Mt. Fuji is July and August. Anytime before or after that, the weather is too unpredictable to be safe. Most of the time in the summertime Fujisan is too shrouded in clouds to see much but right after a storm it is sometimes clear for a couple of days. On a rare clear night one can see steady streams of hikers with flashlights, as hundreds wind their way up the trails. It is said that one has not lived until he has seen the sunrise from the top of Mt. Fuji (but only a fool does it more than once).

At 3776 meters, Fujisan is the tallest mountain in Japan. It is the third tallest mountain in the world that stands alone rather than in a range, and its volcanic origin is most apparent. It is the most photographed mountain in the world and the most photographed object in camera-happy Japan. It is an active volcano that erupts every 200 to 300 years. It has been well over 200 years since it last erupted. Minor tremblings are recorded hourly the year round.

Opening ceremonies take place July first at the Fifth Station starting points for the hiking trails. Tsukamoto-sensei had appointed himself as the official guide, and he, Clyde Hasse, Yumiko and Will left late one August morning. The theory was to take their time, stopping at each station for a rest and a look around. They wanted to make it to the top before nightfall, reserve a place to stay, then get up early enough to find a good place to stand for the sunrise.

Tsukamoto-sensei took small steps, winding back and forth across the trail to make the effort more gradual. Yumiko, and Will followed suit for awhile, then went on ahead as Clyde had done. They found Clyde at the next station already enjoying a cool drink. Tsukamoto finally caught up. As the day wore on, it got harder and harder for Clyde to get back up and start walking again. By the time they reached the top, Tsukamoto had passed everyone and was a good hundred meters ahead. Clyde had a nose bleed, had vomited twice, and was trailing far behind.

Will noticed that the cost of drinks from the machines increased the higher they got up the mountain. One of the canned drinks was called Nude. Another one said, *"Drink this fizzy drink. It will put you in heaven."* Clyde figured they meant to say heavenly, but the Japanese often do not use native speakers when putting things into English, which is why there are so many errors on expensive sign board campaigns, tee shirts and elsewhere around the country. Still, Clyde wasn't so sure he wanted to drink a drink that would put him in heaven—as he wasn't quite ready yet to go. Though, he reasoned, if his altitude sickness got any worse it might be a good idea.

As one travels the trail, one meets people coming the opposite direction quite often. They often greeted the group with "konnichiwa" or "gambatte." Whenever Yumiko asked how far it was to the next station, they would invariably say, "15-funguraidesuyo." ("Fifteen minutes,") regardless of how far it really was.

"tsugimade, kokokara donokuraidesuka? ("How far is the next station?") she'd ask.

"soone, 15-funka, 20-ppunguraikashira." ("Oh, maybe fifteen or 20 minutes.") Fifteen minutes later she'd ask another group how far the next station was. "15-funguraidesu," ("Fifteen minutes,") would be the reply.

When they were nearing the seventh station, Will heard a great deal of huffing and puffing behind him. He looked to see Col. Donelson, the CO of America's Camp Fuji, drenched in sweat as the forty-something year old marine officer *ran* up the trail and passed them. Some time later, younger US Marines also came running past. Then an hour or two later, Col. Donelson came running back down the trail, having reached the top, rested briefly, and turned around—followed somewhat thereafter by his younger retinue of sweating and panting marines as they chased behind their older commander.

Clyde carried a small stick with a war-time hino maru flag attached, which he had stamped at every station along the way. Later they all signed it as a trophy of their adventure. They reached the summit a little after 7:00 PM, made arrangements for a place to sleep, and had dinner at a restaurant at the top. They were able to mail postcards to friends and family postmarked "Mt. Fuji."

The place where they slept was more like a large cubbyhole dug into the side of a cave, with heavy comforters to keep them warm—all sleeping together. They were awakened around 4:00 AM by people getting up and other hikers coming in—having walked all night long.

They got up, had a bite to eat, and went over to the edge of the mountain to watch the sunrise. It was quite beautiful as they had gotten lucky and had a clear day. More often than not hikers are stuck with a view of the sun coming up over a bank of clouds—or of not being able to see the sun at all.

Afterwards they hiked around the crater awhile, then took a different route back down the mountain. It was fun running down areas of loose lava, where they could take giant 20 foot steps. Near the end, however, the ground firmed up. Toes repeatedly jammed into the ends of hiking shoes, giving terrible sets of blisters. Probably the nicest thing of all was realizing when it was all over, and soaking in the Gotemba public onsen, looking at Mt. Fuji across the valley—knowing they had just been to the top of Japan—and knowing they didn't have to do it again.

Watching TV

Watching TV in Japan is different than watching TV in California. Will never went around the channels without seeing at least one cooking show or show about discovering places to eat—or onsens to soak in. Game shows were prevalent. There were some shows similar to US shows, such as a Japanese version of *Who Wants to be a Millionaire?* with Monta Mino, a Japanese look alike to Regis Philbin. Other game shows would stress the Japanese ethic of teamwork, where contestants had to coordinate their efforts to accomplish some feat. Another show had people bringing various relics to be appraised—hoping they had found something worth a fortune. The person would say what they thought something was worth, then find out what the experts had to say.

The news was always something Yumiko and Will would like to watch, though often they missed the early news because of her teaching private English classes which would run late. Will spent quite a long while, guessing what various stories were about, before he discovered that NHK did simulcasting in English. All he had to do was to figure out the right button to push on the remote control.

Will especially liked to see stories about Japanese baseball stars like Ichiro Suzuki in the major leagues. He also enjoyed some of the bizarre commercials—like the one by a moving company where an old woman gets so upset with another worker she starts bumping her with her stomach the way an irritated baseball manager had once bumped an umpire.

The Gotemba Chateau had special antennae, so that it received NHK's BS1 and BS2, often with great old American movies. Sometimes there would be a special campaign, with a week of Audrey Hepburn or John Wayne movies. Other times, they would watch an old Kurosawa flick, or one of the *Tora-san* films (a film series that set the Guinness World Record for the longest running film series with the same actor in the title role—some 48 films). Sometimes they made pilgrimages to where a film was shot, like the time they went to Takahashi.

One September evening, Will turned on the set a bit later than usual—just to see what might be on. There appeared to be some sort of disaster film in progress, but the images seemed very real. A tall building was burning furiously. As he watched, an airplane slammed into another tower of the World Trade Center. Will watched in horror and fascination, as the story unfolded that his country was being attacked by terrorists. He called his dad in California, a former newsman—but his nose for news had already gotten him up and watching early in the morning. The images were sickening, but it was many hours before Will could tear himself away and get a few hours of sleep before getting up to go to work the next day.

Will read the newspaper carefully on the train that morning. It was too soon for anything to be in print. He sat in silence, reflecting on the events he had seen, realizing how far away he was from so many of his friends and family.

Will picked up his backpack as the train crossed Fukikawa, and got off the train like always at the Ooka eki, oblivious to the hordes getting off the train with him and filing down the walkway towards the station house. He was tired, dazed, and still deep in thought, when he heard a gruff voice.

Will was in no mood to deal with the strict old station master who was stopping him again for some infraction or other. He turned back, sighed, and looked at him.

The station master looked at Will. He put the palm of his hand to his heart, then clasped his hands together. He spoke no English, but his sentiments were clear. Will silently nodded thanks, turned, and went to work.

Back home that night and for weeks after Will watched the latest developments. He got numerous expressions of sympathy from many Japanese, often total strangers.

Will called both parents and Ayla Michaela, and then called Walt.

"Good to hear your voice."

"You, too, bro'. Ain't it a pisser?"

"Bad stuff. Real bad."

"Gettin' so nobody's safe anywhere."

"You know, Walt...it sure would be nice to see you sometime. Why don't you come over?"

"Nothin's flyin' right now. Besides, unless you got a Double Lazy R floatin'around over there, I ain't got enough time right now."

"What's that you're lookin' for?"

"I saw this crazy-lookin' branding iron at the Gene Autry Museum and I've been huntin' all over hell and gone tryin' to find me one ever since."

"Ever thought of doing a computer search?"

"Hell, I got no time for them things."

"It could help you out."

"It could turn me into some nerd who spends all his time in front of a screen instead of really livin', too."

"Suit yourself, but I bet you'd have a lot more luck with that than going to antique stores and swap meets."

"Give it up. You can't teach an old dog new tricks."

"I'll make you a bet. If I find it before you do, I'll send it to you—but you have to come over to Japan for a couple of weeks."

"You won't find one over there. What do I get if I come up with it first?"

"I'll pay for it."

"You don't know what you're saying. It'll be expensive."

"I'll win the bet."

"If I had to go over there I'd starve to death."

"You'll get a kobe steak and a lesson in using computers."

"Okay hot shot. You're on."

Yumiko had been upset by the events as well. But soon she was back to normal.

She had a way of flirting with everyone. Rather than making Will jealous, he actually loved to watch her in action. It made her so happy—smiling and chatting, laying a hand lightly on the hand of whomever to whom she was speaking.

The phone rang. Will figured it was Walt trying to wheedle out of the deal. Yumiko answered.

"moshi moshi."

Will waited for the phone. But Yumiko launched into an animated conversation, complete with flirty smiles and exaggerated hand gestures. After awhile Will was guessing either it was a call from an out of town relative or an old friend she hadn't spoken to in awhile.

Finally the call ended and Yumiko hung up the phone.

"Who was that, Yumi-chan?"

"Wrong number."

It took a long time for Will to get to like oolong tea, (Chinese tea), uni, (sea urchin), and natto (putrified soy beans, with a sticky, stringy substance which pulls out in long strands when he tried to eat it). On the other hand, he learned that Yumiko and the rest of her family could not abide the texture of oatmeal, nor the taste of black licorice.

Sometimes if Will got home a bit early, he would make dinner himself. He would make some of his favorite dishes such as chicken Dijon, spaghetti and clams, moussaka, paella, etc. He also tried his hand at shabu shabu, tempura, and yakitori. Sometimes they might have a sauvignon blanc with the fish dishes, or Yumiko's favorite chianti with a meat dish, or Asahi black or Guinness beer, or shochu or sake with Japanese dishes.

Sometimes they dimmed the lights and used candles, and put on a CD with soft guitar music by Anri Shibata, or flute melodies by Hideaki Masago, or selections by the Shamisen Kid. Those were good times.

Occasionally Will would notice Yumiko sitting strangely, looking out the window. It would be too dark to see Fujisan unless there were a full moon. He would lean in to the table to try to see from her angle, then realize she had been looking at her reflection in the glass doors.

"Prettiest girl in the world," he'd say.

Yumiko would giggle.

Yumiko was always on the go. She taught English at four private kindergarten schools four mornings every week, and private or small group lessons in the evening, five days a week. She attended the large shows near the end of the school year put on by the private kindergartens (going up onstage to receive a huge bouquet of roses) while Will sat in the audience next to the local mayor.

She threw Christmas parties for all her students (except the kindergarteners) and usually brought food and gifts she'd picked up on excursions to the United States. She attended clay doll class, singing class, koto class, and played in golf tournaments. Although Will didn't play he would often go to the dinners thrown afterwards at either one of the Hirota's or Kinkabu's. Once again he found himself hobnobbing with mayors, or senior officers from Camp Fuji or the Japanese Defense Forces, and other prominent citizens. Everyone would eat and drink to excess, and everyone went home with at least 2 or 3 prizes—either for their playing skills (the better prizes), or from door prizes.

It was strange how just being a foreigner suddenly made Will important, instead of just being another teacher as he had been in California. Students and parents alike addressed him as "sensei" and usually gave great weight to what he had to say about things.

There were still many things which took getting used to. There would be an old gentleman directing traffic on a hot, humid day. He would wear a full uniform, with long pants and sleeves, a hat, and white gloves. He would bow to each car as it approached and do his best to direct it—often speaking greetings out loud even though the drivers hadn't a chance of hearing a word of it.

Will's legs still cramped up when he sat on a tatami-mat floor at Kinkabu I (Kinkabu II had lower levels for feet, thank goodness). He would end up stretching his legs out, while the other guests pretended not to see.

Japanese toilets were another challenge. There was nothing to rest on—just a porcelain trough to squat over. It was a dangerous proposition even when one was sober, but could easily lead to embarrassing results if one had a few too many shochu or sake servings.

Clyde Hasse had the best story with regards to the Japanese style toilets. He had spent a year teaching English at a school in Shikoku before coming to Nakamura Gakuen. One evening he was invited to a party held at the mayor's office of the town where he worked. Naturally everyone ate and drank until they were ready to burst.

Clyde felt the call of nature, and made his way to the toilet, located right off the main room as they often are. There was a Japanese style commode in the cramped room, up one step. One normally faces towards the commode, away from the step.

Knowing he was well into his cups, Clyde was extra careful to make sure his pants were well out of the way while making use of the facility. When he was done, he couldn't find the toilet paper dispenser. Looking around, he noticed a roll sitting behind him, back by the unbolted door. He stretched an arm back to retrieve the paper, when he suddenly found himself off-balance. The next thing he knew he was doing a wild-eyed backwards somersault off the step, out the door and into the center of the room full of the mayor's surprised guests.

Still clutching the roll of tissue paper, he grabbed the loose pants around his ankles with his other hand to prevent them from tripping him, and made his way, penguin-like back into the little room. It took him a long while to come back out. When he did, no one mentioned a word. It wasn't until years later when the mayor saw him again, that he was asked if he remembered the events of that evening. He pretended not to.

Nightmares and Defragmentation

Anyone who's been up for days in a row knows the importance of sleep. When a computer owner defragments her computer every so often, the computer tries to sort out all the information it's been getting and create some rhyme or reason out of it.

That's what Will's brain did with all the information it acquired during the day when he went to sleep. It sorted out everything he'd seen or experienced then tried to associate it with files that didn't exist. Sometimes he got a glimpse of the process through his dreams. The less references in his life that he had to the information he'd recently been exposed to, the crazier his dreams got trying to put it all together.

In the case of this American who saw billboard after billboard using combinations of kanji, katakana, hiragana, romaji, English and God knows what else, his brain did backwards somersaults. The result was weird, nonsensical dreams he couldn't have begun to imagine on his own.

The whole process would be magnifield another threefold when he had a good helping of gyoza for dinner, accompanied by a few bottles of beer. He would wake up in the morning more tired than when he went to bed, exhausted just from trying to keep up with a mind that was rebelling at the reams of inexplicable babble bombarding it with Dahli-esque images that mutated into one another. It didn't help that they had been further fractured by hot sauces and alcohol.

In conjunction with this, there are different levels of sleep. Someone who has been hypnotized goes into a very deep level of sleep, and awakens greatly refreshed even when the total time of sleep is not as much as normal.

Yet if a person's brain is faced with sorting out the unfathomable, or confronted constantly by a critical boss or jealous co-workers, or with a constant sense of failure as in the case of Aka-chan's son, Bisaku, the sleep is never deep and leaves one with a constant, nagging fatigue. That fatigue saps energy and drive which in turn leads to foolish decision making.

Bisaku felt like he had been getting only a few hours sleep every night. He went to school, and he went to kumon (evening practice school), yet he never seemed to do any better. For awhile he would visit with Will to get help with English or Math. They would struggle, neither being very good in the other's language.

One Saturday, Clyde Hasse told Bisaku that he would be at the school and would spend some time helping him. Together they worked for more than three hours, seldom stopping for a break. Clyde noticed how nervous Bisaku was, and the constant picking at his face. He knew the pressures he was facing. Bisaku was good at identifying trends. He was innovative and creative, but he had little ability in the style of learning that has been mandated by education professionals—that stress identifying and classifying as part of the test-taking education culture of today.

The two finished their work together. Clyde would stay to catch up on some of his own work.

The school seemed almost empty as Bisaku left. He looked across the soccer field to the regular high school that adjoined the elementary. It was not like the modern immersion high school that he attended up on a nearby hill. This was a school where the kids already knew they were destined to the grunt jobs in Japan life. The biggest claim to fame for the school was sports.

As Bisaku casually glanced at the mostly deserted high school, his gaze strayed to an outside balcony high up towards the top of the school. There were more than half a dozen girls standing around. Two of the girls slipped blouses up over their heads. They were braless. He noticed the other girls were already topless. From that distance he could barely make out rebellious smiles on the girls, as they faced one another, and then turned. One of them waved to him.

Bisaku turned forward and kept walking. His eyes did not look back, but his mind would return to that scene many times after that. He wondered if the girls had somehow sensed his awkwardness with the opposite sex. He wondered if they had put on their show to taunt him, knowing he was helpless to do anything about it. He wondered if just the way he walked revealed to everyone that he was a loser in life.

It was difficult for Bisaku to study when thoughts about the incident came to him. Even if he worked very hard, and managed to fool everyone into thinking he had a chance in college, he would then be faced with trying to keep up with everyone in that situation. If he had so much trouble now, how would he be then? He tried to put those thoughts, and the girls out of his mind, but they would come back and haunt him when he least expected it.

In reality, the girls were more interested in impressing one another. They were daring school authority, parents, and society by flaunting themselves in the very place they had to come to school during the week. They had not even known Bisaku was there until one saw him. Several had turned to wave at him, deliberately turning towards him, but he didn't see the rest of them. They turned back to one another, and gave him as much more thought as Mt. Fuji did.

Surf's Up

"moshi, moshi." Will had mastered the art of answering the phone.

"Big News!" It was Chauncy. "There's a major swell pouring through."

Will sat up. "Where did you hear that?"

"The good doctor himself told me. He said he was tooling along the coast near Odawara in his toy car...." (Chauncy always made fun of Dr. Chenoweth's boxy yellow license plate car) "...when a wave came up and almost pushed him off the road."

"Could be gnarly."

"Could be," he said, gleefully. "You in?"

"Hell yes."

"One problem. My wheels are in the shop. Can we take your Honda?"

"Could if I had it. Yumiko's got it. She and her sister went shopping. She's supposed to drop her off and go on from there to her clay doll class."

"Bummer."

"Yeah."

"That's okay. I got an idea. Grab your board and your trunks and meet me out front in an hour."

Will heated up some parafin in an old pot and used a cheap paint brush to smooth wax on a few bare spots on his Hobie Noserider long board. He was beginning to have some second thoughts. It had been well over two years since the last time he surfed, and he wasn't so sure he wanted to go out in an unfamiliar spot, out of practice, on a big overhead day. He was standing out front, wearing his long Hang Ten swim trunks and a shirt, with a towel and wetsuit draped over his board that was leaning on a fence...munching on a bran muffin from the bunch he'd baked the night before.

A horn tooted behind him.

He turned, and there was Chauncy with his head out the window driving as fast as he could in one of the Nakamura red and white kindergarten buses. His head was still clean shaven as he had shaven it just before parent-teacher interviews the week before.

The brakes screeched and he pulled over to where Will stood, amazed.

"Time's a wastin'," he yelled. "Climb in...Surf's up!"

"How did you manage this one?"

"Just gotta know how to read people, s'all."

"I bet. Here," Will said, "Brought you a muffin."

"Thanks. You'll make someone a good wife someday." Will threw his board in and climbed in. Chauncy wheeled the bus in a u-turn, and stomped on the gas pedal. They rounded the corner of the Emperor's Forest, and headed up the hill past Peace Park towards Hakone. Chauncy guided the little bus through tunnels, and around corners while the wheels squealed.

When they got to the coast, they could see large gray swells and windswept white caps. They decided to head north towards Kamakura. Now and then an enormous wave would form, but invariably close out in a long, crushing wall of water. They had their big swell, but it seemed unrideable.

Finally they came to a river mouth marked by gray stones jutting out into the ocean. Some of the waves seemed to hold up, at least a little while. They had come too far not to even venture out, so they donned their wetsuits and began paddling.

Occasionally they did manage to drop into one of the monsters. There would be a hair-raising drop down the face, and then a bottom turn just before the whole wave would crash over and they would be left trying to hold on while bouncing around in a wall of churning white soup. Both of them had gotten into a tube at least once, which, regardless of the outcome made the whole day seem worthwhile. Once they tried to take off on the same wave. It could have been all right – except Chauncy went left and Will went right – directly towards one another. Chauncy tried to kick out and his board went flying. The board hurtled past, the skeg close enough to Will's head to cause his hair to fly up from its wind.

That's when they decided to call it quits and go home.

They paddled up the river a ways, and climbed out past about a half dozen Japanese surfers who had gathered to watch the spectacle. They threw the boards in the back of the bus, and walked over to the locals.

Will tried his poor Japanese. "McDonald's wah doko desuka?"

The boys just looked at him in bewilderment. One of them was thin with longish hair and must have been over two meters tall. "nani?" he said.

Will looked to Chauncy, and muttered, "Every surfer knows the nearest McDonalds."

"Try Ma-ku-do-na-ru-do," he said.

"ah soo," said the tall boy. "Makudonarudo." He pointed further north up the main street.

"arrigatoo gozaimashita."

Then one of them held out a pen and a surf magazine. Chauncy signed "Rob Machado" with a flourish. The boy bowed gratefully and carried his prize back to show the others.

On the outside most McDonalds in Japan look just like McDonalds in the states. However, once inside there are some noticeable differences. For one thing, there is an attentive staff awaiting to serve you. They even bring the food over to your table after you have ordered (but never try to order something which varies in any way from the menu). Although there are restrooms like most McDonalds have, there is also a sink available in the outside eating area for simply washing one's hands before eating. There are also packages of ground sea weed that you can use on your French fries. The teachers each had a burger, fries, and a green tea milk shake.

Back on the highway, they were nearing the cutoff for Hakone when they were pulled over by a patrol car.

Chauncy handled the door control expertly, but pretended not to speak Japanese.

"nihongo sukoshi," Will said. Chauncy gave him a look. Will tried to appear helpful without actually being helpful. Then he had an idea.

"¿Comprende usted español?" Thinking he would be safe in offering to speak Spanish.

"Ah, sí. Hablo un poquito," the policeman replied. Chauncy rolled his eyes.

"What were the chances of a Japanese policeman speaking Spanish?" Will thought, but instead said, "Yo hablo espanol un poquito tambien."

The officer gestured with his hand. "Que pasa aqui?"

"Just tell him the driver got sick," said Chauncy. "I had to take over."

"El"...Will thought for a moment, "...manedor?...estaba enferme. Mi amigo tenia que manejar el autobus."

The policeman nodded. "Y estos platanos de ollas?"

"He wants to know about the surfboards."

"Tell him they're for a science project."

"Estos son para....mmmm...projecto de sciencia."

The officer nodded. He seemed to be mulling over his next question. Finally he turned to Chauncy, and said in flawless English, "Just drive the same speed as the rest of the traffic."

"Yes, sir."

Back on the road Chauncy confided in me that his international license had expired almost a year before. He had tried four times to pass the Japanese driving test. The Japanese have small beautifully designed driving courses to demonstrate one's skills, but one must use the cars provided, get close to the corners before turning, never go over the side of a curb without backing back up over it, and always turn on the turn indicator the moment the test administrator tells one to turn. Chauncy had gotten a hundred percent on the written part (in English), but always failed the driving part. "I've driven all over Japan, from Niigata to Yakushima Island—and I have a good driving record here and in the US. I probably have fewer accidents than any of those dudes testing me. But a driver coming here for the first time, never having driven on the left side of the road before, can rent a car and drive legally while I, with years of experience, can't drive legally. Does that make sense to you?"

Chauncy neglected to say that almost all the other English-speaking countries have agreements with Japan that permits their citizens to use their country's driving licenses to get a Japanese license. The US has no such agreement since it is the individual states that give driver licenses and that would require Japan to have 50 different agreements.

Chauncy dropped Will off at the Gotemba Chateau and headed towards Numazu. Will put his board out on the balcony area of the condo, where he usually kept it. He had time to go downstairs to wash off the salt, get a snack, and send a few emails before there was a call. It was Chauncy. It turned out he got stopped again on the way back to Numazu. When he produced his outdated driver's license, the officer had followed him back to his apartment. There Chauncy had retrieved his work visa, which was also expired. When Yumiko got back Will had to take the Honda and go down to Numazu to bail Chauncy out.

"You owe me bail and a beer."

There have been other foreign teachers in trouble with the law in Japan. There was one case where a teacher got into a fight and was wrongfully accused of starting it (he was later vindicated).

Another time Clyde Hasse was so carried away with the beauty of a temple he was visiting, he threw a 500 yen coin into a special pot before ringing a bell, clapping his hands, and praying. Then he realized he needed some of that money for his train ticket back, and tried to reach in through the grill over the money pot to retrieve it. He wound up in the hoosegow.

Flowers and Time

The passage of time in Japan is often denoted by which flowers are blooming, or in what stage are the foliage of trees. In spring each newscast spends several minutes showing the sakura line in the country—or where the ornamental cherry trees are currently in bloom. This line begins in the warmer, southern part of Japan, and gradually works its way over several weeks to the northern areas of Hokkaido.

Bisaku created his own sakura moving Zen water display. He had painstakingly cut dozens of sakura cherry "blossoms" out of Styrofoam, then dyed them pink. The "blossoms" were slid into the bottom of a flat clear panel filled with water, where they floated to the top. There they were skimmed off, dropped to the bottom and the whole process was repeated.

Television news would show rice being planted at appropriate times during the year in flooded rice paddies.

In June, the hydrangeas bloom—once again starting in the more southerly areas and working their way north or into the cooler, higher elevation areas. Yumiko and Will would visit the Shimoda Hydrangea Festival early in June, Kamakura mid-June, and take the Hydrangea Train near Hakone which goes up the steepest section of mountain track in Japan in late June. The hydrangeas on either side of the train grow higher than the train, and are covered in blossoms. The train stops several times along the way, turns off its lights, and flood lights light up the blue, pink, and white hydrangea blossoms to either side.

In winter they would attend the Narcissus festival on the Izu Peninsula.

Fall

In the fall, leaves turn to yellow and red. It is the most popular time for people to flock to Kyoto, the heart of Japan, or Nara, the soul of Japan. Yumiko and Will loved to go north to Lake Kawaguchi. There was a lane of trees there that always turned bright red. Flood lights were turned on them at night, and photographers vied for top honors in recording their beauty.

The main reason they liked to go, however, was to visit the Ichiku Kubota Kimono Museum.

Coming up from the parking area, one found an ancient, meticulously carved wooden door—standing alone. It was as though Kubota had asked one to come into his realm, which was based upon the nature one had just left. The only difference was that he had provided a frame, so that one saw the natural beauty that was always there through Kubota's artist's eyes.

The museum itself was modeled after a Spanish-styled white cave-like building. There were sliding doors that could be opened to the outside (and were sometimes opened to snow even in winter). There was an inner tea room surrounded by ponds and waterfalls. There was a stage with water running down one side and across it, that was used for special presentations twice a year. An actor wearing a mask and one of Kubota's magnificent kimonos would strut about to the sound of a haunting flute.

Another building had one room designed with natural wood tree trunks and housed a collection of Kubota's beautiful kimonos utilizing the almost lost art of textile dyeing and decorating called tsujigahana (flowers at the crossroads). Will and Yumiko had been marveling at how the material had been gathered into bunches to add texture, when Will took a break and climbed onto a square platform in the center of the room. He excitedly called to Yumiko. When she came up, he pointed to the walls. From a distance, one could make out that the kimonos together actually depicted a single scene of water, islands, woods, hills, and sky—one leading directly into the other, completely surrounding the viewer. Kubota had finished about 38 or 39 kimonos at that time, out of the 80 that should eventually make up Kubota's *Symphony of Light*.

Ichiku Kubota did several kimonos depicting Fujisan. He described seeing the mountain in many different lights. The texture of his materials were perfect for giving the feel to the mottled colors of the surrounding forests near the base of the giant.

Yumiko discovered a path that lead up into a forest along a babbling stream. Up the hill was found a small museum with a sea shell display. Another path lead in another direction along another stream. Following that path Yumiko and Will came to the entrance to a cave. The stream flowed out of the cave. Peering inside they could see statues and altars, dedicated with love to the artist's mother.

In 1995 Ichiku Kubota became the first and only artist for whom the Smithsonian lifted its long honored rule of not showing artists who were still alive. It was highly successful. Another was done in San Diego following his death. His son and daughter have sworn to complete Kubota's unfinished *Symphony*.

Christmas Ski Trip

Less than 1% of Japanese are Christian. When the Nakamura Immersion school first began, foreign teachers were chagrined to find out they had to work on Christmas Day.

Through the years that changed, until the entire staff got more than two weeks off in December. There were staff Christmas pot luck parties where foreign teachers brought traditional foods from their countries. Chauncy would play his guitar and sing Christmas carols, substituting his own lyrics to poke fun at different members of the staff. To the tune of "Here Comes Santa Claus" he sang...

"Here comes Clyde-san,
Here comes Clyde-san,
Right down Gakuen-dori...

Yumiko and Will planned a ski trip with some friends to the Nagano area during the winter break. There were several resorts close to one another, and one could ski there for several days without taking the same run twice.

They stayed at a beautiful ryokan with a lovely ofuro (outdoor onsen hot bath). Whether a bath was to be used by men or women changed constantly, which often made it confusing. It would be easy to understand why a gaijin (foreigner) would go into the wrong one, but somehow it was more often Yumiko who found herself in the men's side by accident.

To Will's relief the ryokan had western style toilets. The first time he sat on one he felt as though someone else had just been on it. It turned out the toilet seat was heated.

The owner/manager had been a member of Japan's Olympic ski team at one time. He would still put on his skis a few times each year, and ski down a nearly vertical wall of icy snow behind his ryokan.

He warned them about the monkeys (the most northerly living primates in the world next to man). If one left his windows unlocked, even on the upper floors, monkeys would come in and wreak havoc with the furniture and one's belongings searching for things to eat or just satisfying their curiosity.

They had enjoyed a full day of skiing when Will decided to take one last run. He took a new chairlift that seemed to keep on going higher and higher than he had expected. When he finally got off he began to wonder if he weren't being a bit rude. It would probably take a long time for him to get back down to the others.

Low clouds began drifting in at that higher elevation and Will could not see very far down the slope. He knew that the hills eventually ended up back at the main road, and that a bus would come along to pick one up wherever he was along the way and take him back to where one was staying.

Will decided to take a short cut. He skied briefly along the ridge, looking for a spot that would take him down to where he figured the road would be. There was a rope going along the ridge, with occasional signs attached to it (though he couldn't read what they said). The fall line looked tricky, which is why he figured the signs were there. But being an accomplished skier Will figured he could save some time. He ducked under the rope and headed down. Big mistake. The signs had been ski boundary signs warning not to go that way—something he was to learn later the hard way.

At first he zig zagged around trees and boulders and headed in the general direction he thought he should be going. But as he traveled on he found some large sections of sheer rock cliff, and noted to himself how back home such areas would have been marked off as dangerous. Finally he found himself flying over an area that looked worse than a Canadian double-diamond run. He hit, fell, rolled several times, and finally stopped himself by digging in with his poles.

He looked in all directions. There was nothing but steep hills. There were no chairlifts in sight. A mist rose up from below. He figured that might indicate civilization—or a way to it.

He made his way down the hill and found the mist was from a geo-thermally heated stream. Japan is the second most seismically active area in the world and there are many natural hot springs. He took his skies off, and walked along the bank. Will expected it would be a matter of minutes before he rounded a bend and saw traffic along the main road. But the deep snow was taking a lot out of him. He was sweating, and at the same time he felt like parts of him were beginning to get quite cold. Being late in the afternoon he was worried that it would get dark before he found his way to the road or that the shuttle buses would stop running.

He took a glove off and felt in his pocket. There were a couple of peppermint candies left over from the restaurant on the mountain where they'd had lunch. He leaned over and gingerly touched the water with the back of his hand. It was quite hot, but bearable. He forced himself to trudge on.

Rounding another bend he still found no trace of the road. There was a wide spot in the river that looked almost man made. It called to him, and he felt himself beginning to feel chilled. Who knew how much further he would have to go or if he was even headed in the right direction?

He decided it was time to take a break. He carefully set down his skies and removed his gloves. He put both hands in the water. They ached from the difference in temperature.

He removed his clothes and tentatively stepped in. Gingerly he eased himself down into the steaming water. It felt wonderful on his tired muscles. His glasses steamed up. He took them off and dipped them in the water. A few moments later they were completely steamed up again. He folded them and set them on a nearby rock.

Will did not know where he was, but for the time being he had his own beautiful, private rotemburo. He closed his eyes and leaned back. He was worried about just how lost he might really be, but the warmth of the water was relaxing, and he felt he had done the right thing taking a break to get warm. It was now early evening and the snow covered beauty of the mountains had given way to a shadowy world. He thought he could see the first planet or star of the night but the steam swirled around and obscured it.

Something moved.

At least, he thought something moved. Maybe the steam was playing tricks on him. The ever-changing mist made it difficult to know if something actually moved or if it was just his imagination.

He thought he saw another movement near the edge of the pond. Then another.

A strange feeling came over him. A feeling like he was being watched. Slowly he turned his head around. A pair of clear brown eyes framed by wild light brown hair were calmly following his movements. They belonged to a macaque (or snow monkey) who was calmly sitting in the water not more than six feet behind Will.

He looked back. More shapes moved at the edge of the pool. "This is interesting," he thought. "At least I have some company."

A scraping sound moved along a rock. "My boots!" A monkey had one of his boots. Then a flash of color as another macaque made off with his parka. He went quickly to the side of the pond. His clothes! The monkeys had grabbed most of his clothes. Something lay on the dirt. He ran out of the water and found a sweater where it had been abandoned.

"Oh my God---my glasses." Clutching the sweater he charged back splashing through the water. The monkey still sat luxuriating in the water where he had left him, and, thankfully, the glasses were still folded neatly on the rock.

Will had been told never to stare at a monkey because they consider it a challenge. The last thing he wanted was a fight with a wild band of Japanese macaques when he had no clothes and no idea how far away he was from any civilization. He put his glasses back on, which immediately fogged up. He found both of his ski boots and both skies further down the river bank. Nothing else remained where he'd left it.

When rescuers came three hours later, he was still in the water clutching the sweater, wearing little more than a sheepish grin. No apologies came from the marauding macaques who evidently felt anything in their territory was fair game. They weren't intimidated by all the action around them. Walt was wrapped in borrowed blankets and transported back to his hotel in a snowmobile.

The hotel's chef prepared a turkey dinner for Christmas Eve from the supplies Will and Yumiko had had sent to him from the Foreign Buyers Club. Yumiko tried to sing a Christmas carol. She would start out with the right tune and words for "Oh Come All Ye Faithful" but somehow always wound up with the tune for "Old Black Joe." There were several toasts to the Japanese macaques.

Outside the snow fell silently, creating a new white wonderland. Begrudgingly, Walt lifted his glass of Christmas amazake. " kampai."

The Bet

"What the hell do you want?"

"Sorry, Walt," Will answered. "I forgot about the time difference."

"It must be four in the morning!"

"Nine PM here. You're just starting the day I'm finishing."

"Christ, Will. This sure hell better be important."

"Imagine a straight line several inches long."

"Imagine my boot in your rear end."

"On the right half above the line is a curving line, making an R on its back—and on the left half the mirror image of that R."

Will could picture Walt sitting up in his bed. "You found it?"

"On the internet, just like I told you I would."

"Damn! How much?"

"My treat. You just have to honor our bet."

"You wouldn't."

"You want a double lazy-R or don't you?"

"Okay, okay—maybe for a few days."

"A month."

"Jesus. I'd starve to death. I can't live on caterpillars wrapped in seaweed."

"Three weeks."

"Two, maybe—but I can't make it until May."

"The sakura will be gone by then."

"Who?"

"Sakura. The cherry blossoms won't be in bloom in May."

"What the hell do I care?"

"Okay. May it is. We'll take in a matsuri or two."

"Only if I get the lazy double-R."

"It's in the mail."

"Jesus, Will. You're really going to hold me to it, aren't you?"

"You bet your boots."

"I'm bringin' my boots. I'm not wearin' any of those bathrobe things...and I don't give a damn if any cherries, daisies or pansies are blooming."

"See you in May."

"Adios."

"Sayonara."

Will put the phone down.

Yumiko was happy when he told her. "He can stay at Tsukamoto's ryokan."

"Good", Will said. But he couldn't help wondering just how good an idea this whole thing would really be.

Calm Before the Storm

Yumiko and Will stood in line at Peace Park, about a mile's walk from Gotemba Chateau, and took their turns ringing the gong to celebrate the new year. They walked along the wide path with the lion statues stylized in the way that various eastern nations do their lions.

Earlier they had attended one of many bonfires in the middle of country intersections, and roasted mochi (pounded rice balls) on long bamboo sticks that arched like fishing poles, like campers roasting marshmallows. Sweet, warm amazaki had been passed around in the frigid air. They had also helped to prepare fish for smoking in outdoor smokers.

The Narcissus Festival on the Izu Peninsula had come and passed, and it was time to gear up for classes again.

Yumiko and Will went shopping at the new Gotemba Outlet stores. Will was always amused by the sweat shirts and tee shirts ordinary citizens wore that had English. One middle-aged, somewhat stout woman was walking with a couple of young children and a baby stroller. Her sweat shirt said, "So many men---so little me."

Another shirt a grandmother wore said, "Too hot for you." Others made no sense at all, with messages like, "Flying books catch nicely", and other such sentiments. One bill board they saw had Kanji, Romaji, Katakana, Hiragana and English—all in the same sentence. Another said, "Drink full, drink happy."

Will was teaching third grade Japanese students math in a foreign language, and was dealing with concepts he hadn't seen in fifth-grade math texts in the US. Often his humor was appreciated, but at other times when he thought he'd said something hilarious there wasn't even a twitter.

One of the parents had decided she was in love with Chauncy, and would dart around corners and trees taking candid photos of him. Chauncy would make some wisecrack and try to figure out another way to shock people around him.

Will had watched one of the most exciting comebacks he'd ever seen in a football game on TV. But in the last few deciding minutes the station cut away to the regularly scheduled programming. In the States there would have been a riot.

Time went on and everyone watched the "sakura line" on the news, as the cherry trees began to blossom further and further to the north. Yumiko and Will and a couple of the Nakamura staff had dinner under the huge flowering cherry trees at the Gotemba Kogen hotel. The blossoms stay only about a week each year.

Hirota Akihiro-san's annual tea ceremony under the spreading sakura blossoms was coming up. The family chipped in together and bought him an ocha wan (tea cup) that a famous ceramicist had made, which scored big points with him. It turned out that he had an extensive collection of tea cups but none from this man who was already being hailed as a national treasure. Akihiro-san's passion for tea cups was similar to Walt's passion for branding irons and old west memorabilia.

West Meets East

Will spotted Walt even before he could make out his face. In his mid-fifties and standing over six feet tall, he wore his cowboy hat and other western garb as he emerged from the plane.

He gave a shout when he saw Will. Older and taller than Will, he came over and lifted him up with a big bear hug.

"Where's that Yummy Yumi?"

"She is shopping with her sister for the ingredients to make your welcoming dinner."

"Uh oh, I'm out of here." He turned and started walking back towards the plane. "Just kidding," he smiled. "I came prepared," he pulled out a bag of beef jerky from his pocket.

There was a bit of a delay as Japanese airport officials mulled over a couple of branding irons (including the Double Lazy R) they found in Walt's suitcase. They must have come up with a satisfactory conclusion as to what they were, because after consulting several higher ups they finally let him pass. Walt insisted on trading in some of his money for Japanese yen (discovering later how hard it was to cash travelers' checks) before loading down Will's poor little red Civic with his luggage, and cramming his long legs into the passenger side.

A couple of times he ducked as they left the airport and headed towards the toll road. "Whole damn country drives on the wrong side of the road."

He liked the roadside stops where one could get off the toll road and get gas or a bite to eat and then get right back on. "Could use some of those in California."

Once off the tomei Walt insisted on stopping to pick up an orchid plant for Yumiko. He mentioned it cost about four times what he would pay at Trader Joe's. While on his way back to the car he disappeared into a doorway. A minute later he had a shop keeper by the arm, and started pointing at something in the window.

He went back in, and again came out carrying a small paper bag. "look at this money," he said, holding up a coin. "It's got a hole in it. I could put it on a necklace. Here, Walt, have a donut."

He handed Will a pastry, then bit into one himself. "Phew!" He spat out the bite. "Some joker put meat and curry inside my donut. I'm gonna straighten this out."

"No, don't, Walt."

"Somebody needs to know about this."

"That's the way they come."

"With meat and curry?"

"Some of them have Azuki in them."

"Afraid to ask, sounds like something you'd say when someone sneezes."

"Beans. Azuki beans."

"In donuts?! What kind of country is this?" He handed Will the bag and started walking. Then, with a matter of fact tone of conviction he muttered to himself, "I'm going to starve."

"They're about to close anyway."

"How do you know?"

"Auld Lang Syne just came on."

"It's Japanese New Year?"

"No. That's what they play to tell customers they're just about to close."

"Should I kiss anyone?"

When they reached Chateau Gotemba Will explained to Walt that gifts, like awards, should be handed to someone with both hands while in Japan. "What's the difference?" he said, handing the orchid to Yumiko. "It ain't that heavy."

Yumiko was delighted with the gift, and greatly fussed over it. Walt gave her a big bear hug. He sometimes complained that she sounded like she was 'talking baby talk' but he always beamed from all the attention she gave him.

Yumiko talked on and on in a very animated way. Walt's smile got broader and broader in spite of himself. "They sure get excited. What did she say?"

"Not quite sure," Will admitted. "I think she's planning your itinerary."

"Don't fuss about me, little lady," he said, beginning to slip into a John Wayne accent. "I'll be just fine."

"You're our special guest. We show you the best gardens and temples in Japan."

"Garden tour," Walt smiled at Yumiko. He rolled his eyes at Will, "Can't wait for that."

Yumiko's sister Sanae and her daughter and family joined them. Yumiko prepared American meatloaf for dinner that night with fresh vegetables accompanied by Asahi Black beer. Walt ate most of everything, although he scraped off the dried seaweed that she had sprinkled on top for kakushiashi (special secret taste).

At first Yumiko's niece's children bowed and acted polite, but after dinner they couldn't help staring and trying to touch the turquoise stones on Walt's ring, bow tie and belt buckle. He chuckled and showed them how to make it look like they were taking off their thumbs. Before too long they were wrestling and tickling on the living room rug and sofa. Little Hiroshi squirmed and laughed and threw up on the couch.

The next day they got up early and drove down to take a ferry across to the Izu Peninsula. They saw an ancient gold mine, and the world's largest floral faced clock (according to the Guinness Book of Records). They traveled down to the place where one of the Nakamura teachers told Will he liked to take his son canoeing. They boarded a boat that took them inside a sea cave where it turned around and came back out, and hiked up a hill to see a special orchid garden that even seemed to impress Walt.

Then they drove on down the peninsula taking the Kawazu-Nanadaru bridge that looped around and around like a corkscrew. They visited Shimoda briefly, and ran into a mutual friend of Tsukamoto-sensei and Yumiko. He was some sort of town official, and seemed especially interested in how tall Walt was—indicating with his hands, then bowing and smiling towards Walt. Yumiko grew very animated while talking with him. Later Will asked what they had spoken about.

"I cannot tell you now," she said. "But if it happens it will be a very big honor. Very big."

"What is it?" Will insisted.

"It is secret. I cannot tell you until it is official. You must be hush hush about it."

"How can I be hush hush if I don't know what it is?"

"Walt will be very, very big."

"He already is."

"Important big."

"Why would he be important big?"

"Because," she said.

"Because why?"

"I cannot say. It's hush hush."

They stopped at a kaiten sushi restaurant. As the food moved past on a conveyor belt, Walt would pick up a plate, smell it, roll his eyes and put it back. Eventually he tried a few things. Yumiko ended up with more than twice as many dishes as Walt and Will put together. Will never could figure out where she put it all.

They took a different route back, without using the ferry boat. They saw green tea plants (like camellias) growing, rice fields, mikans (like tangerines), and a shady canyon where they grew wasabi (kind of a green horse radish). Walt liked many of the hot wasabi products, and even tried the wasabi ice cream. "Not as hot as Texas chili," he said, "but not bad."

They made it back to Gotemba just in time for a special dinner at Hirota's in Walt's honor.

It was extra busy that evening, as they revealed a new creation by Bisaku that had been funded by Akihiro-san. There were five panels side by side along a wall of the western dining area. The center and two end panels had uniform streams of water flowing downwards. There were occasional volcanic rocks interrupting the flow but the water eventually found itself in more clear plastic channels. The two inner panels were completely filled with water. They too had volcanic stones in them. Only in these panels there were streams of bubbles uniformly headed upwards, until they came in contact with the rocks and made their way around. In a way the display was like a moving Zen garden hanging on a wall. Akihiro-san had mixed feelings about it, but he knew that Bisaku was proud of his work and the controversy about it had brought in a few more customers just to see it.

Bisaku would come into the restaurant and begin to bus tables, just so he could hear the reactions of customers. Customers would wonder why he grinned when they talked about the strange wall display never suspecting he had been the artist who created it.

Walt tried to hold his chopsticks together and scoop up his food, but wasn't getting the quantity per bite he was used to. Finally he managed to stab through a small, stiff fish. He picked it up and looked at it, eye to eye. "This is the moment I dreaded before coming here." Then, to the amazement of all, he bit the head off—then ate the whole thing. Yumiko clapped.

Walt loved the white meat chicken yakitori (but not the livers). He even liked a special concoction Akihiro-san created of eel and Korean kimchee.

There was a beautiful arrangement of flowers on the table. Tsukamoto-sensei attended, and brought a beautiful five foot long noren depicting a kabuki player carrying a parasol as a welcoming gift. Walt looked befuddled but thanked him. "Very big man soon," Tsukamoto told him, chuckling and patting him on the shoulder.

Yumiko put her finger to her mouth, "Sssshhh Sensei."

After the meal they all thanked Akihiro-san who was rightly proud of the feast he had prepared. Caught up in his success he asked Yumiko to invite Walt to attend a tea ceremony he would be performing in a couple of days. Will did everything he could to get Walt's attention to tell him to excuse himself.

"Tea isn't my thing, really. I'm more of a beer man—but what the hell. When in Rome, right?"

Will sighed. The die was cast.

Sadoo II

Caesar crossing the Rubicon did not have any greater trepidation than Will had on the way to Akihiro's tea ceremony. He wanted to stay in the back out of the way, but figured he might have to be handy in case of an emergency.

When Walt made his entrance he seemed strangely happy. He was wearing his best "western" garb—leather boots, blue jeans, belt with a huge buckle, open necked square dancing shirt draped with a squash blossom necklace and a neckerchief, and of course, his Stetson hat. Other guests moved towards him and bowed. Walt would give them a booming "Howdy" and stretch out a large hand. Most of the guests would hesitate, then shake hands with him, then bow again.

When Walt came to Yumiko he picked her up and wheeled her around once in the air. "Howdy, Sweet-thing."

"Walt-san," she said, looking about but smiling in spite of herself. "That is not proper. You smell like beer."

"I like that Asahi brew," he said. Then he slipped out of his phony Texas accent and into a posh English accent, holding an imaginary tea cup with a pinky extended into the air. "Tea time. I'm now ready for my spot of tea and crumpets."

A beautiful young, slim girl in her twenties, exquisitely dressed in a kimono with elaborately coiffed hair came to guide Walt to his place of honor. Walt caught Will's eye. "Hubba hubba, get a load of this baby, would ya."

Akihiro-san was still busying himself with preparations, and had not seemed to take notice of Walt yet. Walt was seated on the extreme end, shokyaku, the place of highest honor. That was even worse than where Will had been seated for his first tea ceremony. At least Will had a chance to observe someone before he was served. Walt would have no one going before him.

"Can't they afford chairs?" Walt muttered. "Guess I gotta do this Apache style." He sat down and folded his legs across, grabbing his boots with his hands to pull them up into place—yoga-like.

Sakai Tamatsu, the mayor of Susono, wearing a beautiful black kimono, bowed to him, and sat down next to him in the jiyaku position, properly placing himself on his knees. "ohaiyo gozaimasu." ("Good morning.")

"Right back at you," said Walt, winking and tipping his hat.

Six other guests took their places at a right angle to Mayor Sakai-san and Walt. The mayor looked to be in his 60's, with gray hair and bushy gray eyebrows. He knew the formalities of the situation, but there seemed to be a hint of amusement in his eye if one looked closely enough.

The same young woman who had seated Walt returned taking small measured steps. She was carrying a tray with eight strawberry colored sweet rice balls, each beautifully arranged on a leaf. She gracefully knelt in front of Walt and held out the tray with both hands.

"Hmm. That's interesting. Dessert first."

Walt reached out and took hold of the tray. The woman's eyes widened in terror, like a deer that's spotted a pack of coyotes. For a moment she resisted Walt, having never been faced with such a situation.

Mayor Sakai-san caught her eye and gestured calmly to her with one hand, and with the other helped to take the entire tray and set it down in front of Walt. He then indicated for the young woman to go back for another tray.

"Cute little buggers, aren't they?"

In a minute or so the young woman returned with a different tray, this time with seven of the pink delicacies. She approached the mayor who withdrew a napkin from his obi, bowed to her and removed a wagashi from the tray with a small fork. She bowed and continued on to the other participants who each took one of the mochi treats.

Walt was eating one of the mochi balls. "Not much appetite, huh? Don't blame you." He examined the morsel more closely. " I don't usually go around eating leaves. These little marshmallow doodads are okay, I guess." Walt crammed a couple more into his mouth.

Akahiro-san began the elaborate ceremony for which he had trained much of his later life. He carefully folded his napkin-like fukusa and tucked it into his obi. He warmed a beautiful ocha-wan (tea cup-- like a bowl), with warm water. He carefully measured green tea powder with a bent piece of bamboo.

Walt looked around, oblivious to the performance. "Nice weather we are having."

The mayor didn't miss a beat. His English was good. "Yes. Rittle rain, rately."

"You mean, little rain, lately," Walt corrected.

"Yes. Rittle rain."

Walt gave a sour look, then shrugged. "Takes awhile... Glad it doesn't take me this long to make coffee in the morning." He crammed another one of the rice delicacies into his mouth. "Mushy little devils," he managed with a full mouth, "ain't they?" Then swallowed. He licked the powder off his fingers. He held out the tray to Mayor Sakai-san. "Sure you don't want another one?"

The mayor politely declined.

Akihiro-san was proud of his ability as a tea master. He was even more proud of his beautiful collection of tea bowls. They came in different colors and styles. Some were from modern ceramicists and others were quite old.

Now Akihiro-san selected one of his favorite ocha-wan bowls to make tea for the guest of honor. It was green with an irregular lip around the top, and large drips frozen in time along the sides. He added the tea and hot water, and stirred it thoroughly with the little bamboo wisk that reminded Walt of an old style shaving brush. Then he carefully turned the cup around and set it down for the young woman to take.

The woman picked up the cup, turned it, and carried it over to Walt. The mayor held up his hand, and indicated she should bring it to him instead.

She hesitated, then knelt before the mayor and presented him with the cup. He took it from her then set it to one side. He turned to Walt, and bowed low. "osakini."

Walt looked embarrassed. He spread his fingers and waved his hands around in small circles towards the mayor apologetically. "I don't do the bowing thing."

In Akihiro's mind, a small frog pushed underwater.

The mayor raised up and faced forward. He gave a look sideways to Walt that said, "Watch and learn."

The mayor then picked up the cup, and turned it half around in two movements. He lifted it up above his head, aimed towards Akihiro-san, and said, "otemai cho-dai, itashimasu."

He drank all the tea in precisely three and a half sips, loudly slurping the last one.

Walt gave him a look half curious, half of disdain. "That can't be polite."

Mayor Sakai-san set down his tea bowl, then immediately picked it up again. He gave a look to Walt to make sure he was watching, then he looked closely at the tea bowl, examining it from all sides. Finally he held it up, looked across at Akihiro-san, and said, "totemo ii ocha-wan, ii desu ne?"

He then turned it half way around in two movements, wiped the lip with his finger, wiped his finger on his napkin, and set the bowl in front of him. He looked at Walt to see if he had gotten it.

Then the young woman brought a bowl to Walt. Will crossed his fingers. Yumiko saw what Will did and gave him a little frown. She looked back at Walt. Then she decided to cross her fingers, too.

The woman knelt down and set the bowl in front of him. "Thank you, honey," Walt drawled.

Walt reached for the bowl. "Damn, that's hot." He picked it up. "Kinda skimpy." He shrugged. He looked at Mayor Sakai-san. "Here's mud in your eye." Then he looked at Akihiro-san. "Cheers." He downed the cup, slurping loudly. He stopped, saw a little more, and finished it off. Then he belched.

"I heard that was polite to do over here" he said proudly. "Or is that Arabia? " He ran his tongue over his teeth. "Kinda bitter. Don't know what the fuss is all about. Sure don't beat a cuppa java." He looked at the bowl that had large drops frozen along the sides. He touched one of the drops. "Kinda sloppy with the shellac here. Seen better cups made by kiddiegartners."

Still holding the bowl in a careless manner Walt leaned over to the mayor. "How'd I do?"

"Perfect."

A frog blew up its throat like a balloon. One eye closed while the other bugged out, then that eye closed and the other one bugged out.

Walt looked back at Will. Then, loud enough so he could hear, "See that? The big cheese said I was perfect." He smiled, tossed the bowl up, caught it, and set it upside down in front of him, pleased with himself.

Later in the ceremony when the young girl tried to collect the bowls, Walt said, "Let me help you, darlin'." He rose with her and before anything could be done about it, a prized cup of Akihiro-san's collection hit the ground with a loud cracking sound.

"Sorry about that. I'll pick up another one at the store for you."

Akihiro-san turned red. The frog froze.

x x x x x x x x x x x x x x x x x x x x x

An American fisherman got blown off course in a storm, and happened to land on the shores of Japan. Unlike his companions, he had escaped a watery grave and kissed the white sand of the beach when he landed. His hopes rose when he found signs of civilization—cultivated fields, statues, temples and sturdily built dwellings (at least he had not landed in a place of savages who wielded spears or bows and arrows).

Eventually two figures came towards him. They spoke a strange language and chattered excitedly to one another. He gestured with his hands towards his mouth indicating his need for fresh water. The small, yellow-brown figures looked at him through eyes that had an extra fold of skin. They stared, then looked at one another. Then they turned and headed back the way they had come.

The fisherman struggled to keep up with them, but he was far too weary. By the time he reached the edges of a small town the two had disappeared. More villagers saw him, and a stir went up. Children ran from where they had been playing to shyly peer around corners. One boy could not contain his curiosity. He approached the fisherman, tentatively reached out and touched his sunburned skin, just before his mother snatched him up uttering a torrent of admonishments.

Some people backed away from the strange foreigner, watching as though he were a wild beast that could attack them at any time. Then through the streets another man strode towards him with purpose. He had an air of authority about him. Behind him trailed the first two, walking in hurried but smaller steps, keeping up but not too closely.

The man's clothes and hairstyle were different than the others. He wore two slightly curved swords in scabbards at his side, a short and a long one. Villagers quickly moved out of his way when they saw him approaching or prostrated themselves, bowing low until their heads touched the earth.

The fisherman stopped. He hoped this man would act decisively to help him.

The samurai was of a different class than the villagers. He was used to being obeyed without question or hesitation. He realized this man before him was one of the foreigners he had been warned about by the Bakufu. No foreigners were to enter other than a few traders from Portugal, and they were confined to a small island off of Nagasaki, allowed to make one or two pilgrimages a year to Edo where they could trade goods from around the world for Japanese fineries.

The samurai spoke firmly in good Japanese. He spoke slowly and not unkindly, but made it known the man was not wanted in the village under his protection.

The fisherman realized he had a problem. Using his own English language he gestured towards the sea. "I come from a land far across the ocean," he said. My ship and comrades have been lost, and I need your help to survive and to find my way home."

The swordsman listened to the strange sounds emanating from the figure with the strange clothing. He took in every bit of information available to him. He held up a hand, then gestured towards the ocean. His tone was more forceful this time. He knew that it had not gone unnoticed that this man had not shown him proper respect. He had not bowed or kept his head lower, not even had he done the slightest nod.

The fisherman looked at him, then looked at the ocean, then looked back at him in disbelief. His tone of voice was incredulous. "Surely you would not begrudge a man some water and vittles? I've survived a nightmare of a storm and do not ask for much."

Now the samurai could feel the stares burning into the back of his neck. Surely this was the evil that foreigners bring. This was an example of the very reason why they had been driven from the country, the reason Japanese must be ever vigilant that they not enter and corrupt the established way things were done in Nippon.

He knew he must act quickly to demonstrate that even foreigners must honor the ways of the caste system. The samurai reached for the hilt of his sword. His first impulse was to demand the man bow to him immediately and show his obedience. But as soon as he touched it, he knew what he would have to do. He realized the man would not understand a word he would say, that he would not bow down, and that since he had already touched his sword he must follow through with it to its logical conclusion.

The fisherman's eyes widened. "What the...?"

Before he could finish, the sword had left its scabbard. In one fluid movement the samurai sliced through the fisherman's throat, separating his head which fell backward and landed without a bounce in the deep sand, cocked at an angle with his eyes towards the cloud covered sky. His body collapsed. Blood gushed from the neck and bloomed through the sand, pumping and pushing a circle continually outwards, saturating and clumping the absorbent grains together.

It had been this way for others who had been stranded on the shores of the Japans. The same was true even for some Japanese fishermen who had themselves been blown off course to foreign lands. Upon returning they had been deemed impure from their exposure to foreigners, and had suffered a similar fate to the American fisherman at the hands of their own countrymen.

This had been the way since the first Shogun, the great Tokugawa had decided to rid Japan of all the missionaries working so hard to save the "heathens" of Japan. He was aware of the synchronous relationship the church had with colonialism. He saw the subjugation of people in China and Korea, and declared that would not happen in Japan. Thousands of missionaries were driven away. Those who would not go were unceremoniously put to death. Perhaps that may be why today more than 90% of Korea is Christian (with the largest church in the world), yet less than 0.7% of the Japanese population are Christian.

Although Tokugawa befriended a foreigner himself (British subject William Adams was given the status of samurai), he was thorough in ridding Japan of missionaries. It is not known if Tokugawa was aware of the influence of the church in places like Mexico and Central and South America, or of the enslavement of Africans or the genocide of Native Americans that occurred in the Americas. But what he did know kept a policy of isolation in place for about 250 years.

Japan had learned something of the vastness of the United States from Katsuo Kaishu, who managed to sail one of Japan's coastal fishing vessels to California where he spent quite a while in San Francisco learning about western culture. He eventually became the father of Japan's modern navy, partly with the help of Ryoma Sakamoto who wrote one of the first drafts of a constitution for Japan.

It's interesting to note that one of the first people to successfully enter Japan without separating from his head was a half-Native American named Ranald McDonald (no relation to the hamburger icon). He had heard strange tales about an exotic Japan while growing up on the Pacific Coast near what is now Seattle, Washington (named for a great Native American chief). Perhaps the only reason McDonald was successful was that the first Japanese he ran into were members of Japans only native (and also persecuted) people, the Ainu. They are hairier and lighter skinned than most modern Japanese and definitely come from a different gene pool (see the Smithsonian Ainu museum online).

Ranald McDonald's father was a Scot employed by the Hudson Bay Company, and his mother was a daughter of a chief in the Northwestern territory. Well-educated in an ivy-league college, Ranald eventually became a harpoonist for whaling ships (about the time Melville was writing Moby Dick). Whaling ships routinely hunted whales around Japan and McDonald hatched a plan to find out about the exotic land. He asked the captain if he could exchange his share of the profits for a long boat and supplies and be left off near the Japans (the ship he was on still holds the record for most whale oil taken on a voyage).

The captain reluctantly honored the agreement and dropped him off. McDonald waited a few days until the ship had left the vicinity, then headed into an island. He practiced turning his boat over to make it seem more realistic. He never ran into the people who were on that first island (probably lucky for him), and sailed north to what is now known as Hokkaido. There he turned his boat over, but accidentally lost most of his supplies. The one thing he did manage to save was a trunk full of Bibles (another thing that could have gotten him into trouble if it hadn't been for the Ainu finding him first).

McDonald spent most of a year in Japan, and is considered the first English teacher there. It was only because Japan's best language scholars met him that they were able to communicate with Commodore Perry when he came several years later in his black steam/sailing ships with powerful cannons to open Japan up to trade with the US.

The Black Ships Festival

Will took great pains to coach Walt in the proper etiquette for using the ofuro (or daiyokujo—public bath) downstairs at the Gotemba Chateau. They took the elevator downstairs, passed the beer and sake vending machines, passed the workout/massage room, and entered one of the two public baths (which would trade Wednesdays between men and women). They took shaving items in small plastic buckets, carried towels, and wore robe-like yukatas and sandals.

"It's important to sit on a low stool and thoroughly clean yourself before getting into the bath," Will told him.

"What's the point of taking a bath if you're already clean?" Walt responded.

"And never have any soap left on your body when you enter the bath."

"It ain't a bath without soap."

They slid the door open. A neighbor was just leaving. As he passed he bowed slightly and said, "shitsure shimasu."

"Same to you, too," smiled Walt. Then to Will, "What's that mean?"

"I'm not really sure exactly what it means," he said, "but people say it when they walk by or leave or anything. I think it roughly translates to, 'Humbly excuse me for being in space near you with my unworthy body', or something."

"Well, hell. It's their country. Why do I need to excuse them for being here?"

They walked through the door into a steamy room. The ofuro looked like a large pond, with a small waterfall, and brown rocks set in cement. A window ran the length of the far wall that showed a small garden open to the sky a floor above. A solid wall behind the garden lead up to a field above. In winter when it snowed the garden was covered in a delicate blanket of white. This time of year was always warm.

They went to a small rock-basin and used a bamboo dipper to douse themselves with chilly water. Then they inched themselves into the extremely hot water, and lowered themselves gradually down until their shoulders were covered.

"You know, Yumiko says that Akahiro-san is still upset about his chaki."

Walt dripped water on his head, like Marlon Brando in ***Apocalypse Now.*** "His chucky?"

"His tea cup."

"I said I'd buy him another one. Hell, I'll even get him some tea bags to save him all that trouble he goes through."

"She said it cost almost a quarter million yen."

"How much is that in real money?"

"More than $2000."

Walt whistled. "For that little thing? The sides weren't even straight. It looked like some kid made it who didn't know when to stop with the shellac."

"It was his favorite, and he was honoring you by letting you drink from it. He has been looking in every ceramic and antique shop from here to Mishima trying to find a suitable replacement, but hasn't come up with anything."

"Hells bells. Why would anyone get so excited about a tea cup?" He acted disgusted, (but Will could tell he felt badly about the situation).

Walt scratched himself, and looked down at nothing. It bothered him that he didn't understand. Part of him felt put upon from even having to be in such a strange place, and part of him wanted to just get out and go— anywhere as long as he didn't have to feel like he was always doing the wrong thing all the time.

"We better get out. We've got a long drive ahead of us."

"Where we headed?"

"Shimoda again. We'll stay in the oldest building in town. One of three that was left standing after a tsunami hit over a hundred years ago while a ship from Russia was visiting. They were there trying to do their own black ship thing about half a year after Perry. According to Yumiko there's big doings tomorrow."

"Yeah, I know there's something going on. I'm actually doing something myself, I think."

"Really?

"Yumiko and your teacher friend talked to me. They were very happy about something, but told me not to tell anyone."

"About what?"

"Wish I knew. I talked with them, but I'll be damned if I know what it was about."

They climbed out and dried off. Refreshed from the bath, they got dressed, threw overnight bags into the Honda—then sat there watching the small color TV that folded out from the dash board until Yumiko came out to join them. Then they headed to Shimoda.

x x x x x x x x x x x x x x x x x x x x x x x

The ryokan was simple, old and charming. The outside had the Shimoda traditional nameko walls (white lattice grid over black slate). Beds were the traditional pads rolled out on tatami-covered floors after dinner, and toilets were the traditional Japanese ones.

After finding the hotel they took a stroll along a canal. They saw the museum dedicated to the Black Ships (one wing, seemingly with no rhyme or reason being devoted to ancient sexual objects like stone dildos shaped like penises or vulva). They met up with Tsukamoto-sensei, his wife, and a couple of Shimoda officials—and went out for a splendid meal at one of the many fine restaurants.

In another month or so the hydrangea would be in full bloom in the hill park.

x x x x x x x x x x x x x x x x x x x x x x x

The next morning Will awoke to the smell of salt air drifting in through the windows. His body ached from sleeping on the hard tatami mat that had only a few blankets thrown over it. He stretched and looked around at the room.

Yumiko had gotten up earlier, dressed, eaten in the common dining room and gone out. She left a note telling him he would be on his own all day, but predicting something "...would happen most important and most wonderful this special day."

Will smiled at the wording of the note, scratched the stubble on his face, and decided he and Walt would use the time to go to a floating aquarium around the corner from the bay, where people could see tank exhibits and go swimming with dolphins.

He performed his morning ablutions and made his way to Walt's door. He knocked. There was no response. Gently he pushed the door open. The room was messy, and bedclothes lay on the floor. Walt wasn't there.

He went into the dining room and had a breakfast of salmon, salad and green tea. The owner had made a pot of coffee (possibly because of the Americans). Walt poured himself a cup and walked outside. He stretched and looked at the old town, and the street stretching toward the bay.

Shimoda is a port town. Fishing boats are tied to docks. Near the outside edge of the bay was a large US destroyer at anchor. There were also two old black ships that were chugging along towards the harbor.

The town was teeming with tourists, Japanese and others—even more than usual. Bits of German, English, and something Will figured to be a Scandinavian language floated to his ears from groups making their way to the main thoroughfare along the waterfront. There were families with children, aunts and uncles, friends and neighbors smiling, laughing, but generally headed in the same direction.

Will brought his cup inside, took one more gulp, thanked the owner and headed back out. Somewhere he heard music playing. There was marching music and the sound of drums. It seemed like it was coming from near the water.

Will fit into the flow of people walking along. A small girl twisted out of the grasp of her father and went back to a shop window that had a Hello Kitty doll and phone. She stomped her feet and shrieked in misery when she was pulled away, then was lifted up to her father's shoulders. The man was probably a salary man who had gotten away for an extended weekend. He was thin, wore glasses and had on a shirt that was too big for him. His wife scolded two other young children and pulled them along down the street.

Will turned a corner and found a full-fledged parade moving along. There were US sailors in full dress uniform marching in a column, followed by Japanese wearing traditional clothing from the 1800's, complete with kimonos and shaved head hairdos. Too bad Walt was missing it, he thought, although he wasn't sure if his brother would really appreciate it or not.

Then came a Japanese man dressed as Commodore Perry. He had on a traditional military uniform and a shock of red hair. A taller man, dressed as Townsend Harris walked along, waving now and then and throwing kisses to the crowd. There were several men who appeared to be high-ranking Japanese officials, and two women dressed like geisha.

As the last of the procession passed, Will fell in with a noisy crowd that had decided to follow. They wended their way through the streets of Shimoda, turned, and found their way up a hill to the Ryosenji Temple.

Some of the parade disbanded, while others took up positions on the temple grounds. Taking center stage were the Japanese officials, Commodore Perry, Townsend Harris, and the two geishas.

Will caught his breath. He made his way in for a closer look.

"Howdy folks. Thanking you kindly." The voice was unmistakable. The tall man portraying Townsend Harris with the long sideburns and nineteenth century suit was none other than his brother, Walt.

Okichi Saves the Day

"Welcome to all," it was the man portraying the Japanese translator, Takichiro Moriyama. He continued in wavering English, looking at notes he had written.

"We are honored by your plesence here today." He bowed first to Commodore Perry, then to Townsend Harris. Commodore Perry clicked his heals together, then returned a deep bow. Townsend Harris (Walt) tipped his hat.

"Today we cerebrate the coming of the American Brack Ships, the opening of Japan to the world, and the signing of trade treaty."

"I am honored by the hos'tality of Japahnese people," said the Japanese Commodore Perry.

"This is an important, historical occasion," said Townsend Harris (Walt). "You people should never forget this." The sound system made a deafening sound as microphones created feedback.

"Thank you vely much," said Translator Moriyama. "And now, it is my great preasure to introduce chief negotiator for Japan, the honorable Daigaku Hayashi."

At that moment, a door to the temple slid open wide and a man splendidly dressed as Hayashi Daigaku-no-kami Razan, the nineteenth century political theorist, emerged.

Will immediately recognized him as Mr. Akihiro Hirota. The old man came bustling out with a wide smile on his face.

"yokoso irrashaimashita. kono rekishitekini juuyoona toki….. naniii?? ano bakaga, konna tokorode nani shiterunda?" ("Welcome and warmest of greetings on this auspicious occasion—what the hell is this idiot doing here?")

A gasp rose up from the crowd. Akihiro-san froze, his eyes widening, brows arching.

Takichiro Moriyama translated. "Warm greetings to you on this occasion." Then he looked up at Hayashi-san (Akihiro-san) with befuddlement, then looked back down at his notes, then back at Akihiro. His mouth opened, and his eyebrows wavered.

"It's the old fart himself!" said Townsend Walt, recognizing Akihiro-san.

"ano bakaga ittai dooshite kokoni irunda?!" ("What moronic jack-ass brought this numbskull here?!") Akihiro-san was now bright red.

Takichiro-san turned pale. His frightened eyes turned from Akihiro-san to Walt, but he was unable to mutter anything.

"Choto mate kudasai", (Just a moment, please). it was Yumiko dressed in a geisha outfit portraying the ill-fated, teen aged Okishi (later to briefly be Townsend Harris's reluctant helper and, according to some, mistress).

She turned to Walt. "He says he was surprised to see the esteemed Mast-san here today."

"Well he don't seem so damn happy about it."

"Excuse, please." She turned to her father. "otoosama. Waruto-san wa, konnani subarashii gyojino bade otoosamani aukotoga dekite, totemo yorokonde irunoyo. ("Dearest father. Walt-san is so happy to see you here at this most important event.")

"ano bakaga zenbu dainashinisuru... Tatoe jibunno inochiga kakatteitemo, tadashii kotoga dekin yatsudakarana!" ("That idiot ruins everything. He couldn't do anything right even if his life depended on it!")

"That old geezer's going to give himself a heart attack. What's got his dander up, anyway?"

"Father, I mean, Daigaku Hayashi-san says you have done a remarkable job. You look just like the great Townsend Harris."

"Miseteyaruwa." ("I'll show you what you can do!") Akihiro-san grabbed a sheet of paper that was to be part of the treaty. He stood with a wide stance and deliberately tore it apart. Then he wadded it up into small balls of paper.

The other Japanese officials looked aghast.

Akihiro-san held the pieces of paper in one hand, turned around and pretended to drop them from his behind like a horse relieving itself. "kono kamikire, umano ketsukara kureteyaruwa." ("Here is your damn treaty, Horse's ass. Choke on it.")

"What the..." stammered Walt. "Now that <u>can't</u> be polite."

Will wondered if he shouldn't step in.

"Walt-san," said Yumiko. "He says he admires your cowboy ways, and hopes that some day you will teach him how to ride a horse like you."

"Really? I was gettin' ready to knock the old boy on his ass."

"otoo-san. Waruto-sanwane, dooshite otoo-sanga sonnani okotteirunoka, wakatterutte. Jibunga otoo-sanni shitakotoni taishite, mooshiwakenaitte. demo, shimodano hitotachi minnani ikario butsukenaide hoshiitte. Konna tokikoso, otonagearu koodooo surubekidato, watashimo omouwa." ("Father. Walt says he understands why you are upset with him and he's sorry for what he did. But he feels you should not take it out on the people of Shimoda. You must face the situation like reasonable men.")

The old man considered for a moment. "Warutoga hontoni soo ittanoka?" ("He said all that?") He sighed. "jibundatte Shimodani kitemade konna kotowa shitakunakatta. Shimodano hitotachiwa minna ii hitotachibakaridakara." ("I did not want to bring dishonor on Shimoda. These are good people.")

Yumiko, (touching Walt's arm), "Father really appreciates all your efforts to introduce western culture."

"I don't do a lot of riding...I know a couple of rope tricks."

Akihiro-san bowed to the crowd. "taihen omigurushii tokoroo omiseshimashita... otonagenai koodoo owabishitai.." ("I'm sorry for my behavior...... I'm sorry for inflicting this idiot on you.")

Takashiro-san looked like he would faint.

Walt raised his hand towards Yumiko-Okichi-san. "Tell him I'm just here to do a favor. If he can apologize and behave himself I'll go on with this shindig."

"Waruto-sanga otoo-sanni ayamaritaitte itterundakedo, otoo-sanga yurushitekureruka dooka shiritaisooyo. soo sureba shikitenga tsudukerareu deshoo?. ("Walt-san apologizes to you. He wants to know if you will forgive him so that the ceremony can proceed?")

Akihiro-san weighed his options. He tugged on the sleeves of his costume. "yurusuto itteagenasai. shimodano hitotachino tameni, shikiteno tsudzukerunda." ("Apology accepted – only for the people of Shimoda.")

Yumiko to Walt; "He says he admires your spirit. He would be honored to continue."

"Glad to see he's come to his senses."

The two men faced one another with uneasy glances. Akihiro-san bowed. Walt looked around, then did a kind of clumsy bow.

The other officials looked at one another, then hurriedly found more paper and a quill pen. There were no more problems other than Townsend Harris misspelling his own name.

Okichi had saved the day.

Otoko wa tsurai yo

Back at the ryokan that evening, Will showed Akihiro-san a branding iron that Walt had brought along. Akihiro was fascinated with it, but had no idea for what it was used. Yumiko found a restaurant owner who heated the iron up on an iriori and then "branded" some kobe steaks for dinner. It impressed Akihiro-san so much that he branded some fish steaks later back at Hirota's for some of his regular customers.

Walt had asked Yumiko to write down in Japanese the type of tea bowl he had broken. He told her he would be going out of town. He took his small, old suitcase, leaving the larger one for Will to take back to Gotemba.

"What do you mean he told you he was going out of town?" Will said when he found out.

"He said to tell his little brother not to worry, he had something he had to do."

"He can't speak diddly in Japanese."

"Neither can you."

At least I know "Toire wa doko desuka?"

153

"He's a grown man."

"eki wah doko desuka?"

"He won't have too much trouble."

"If I know Walt, he's already in trouble." They looked at one another with growing concern.

The next day their group, minus Walt, traveled back to Gotemba, and settled into life and their usual identities.

A few days later some of the family had found their way to Hirota's in Gotemba. There were only two customers left, finishing up their lunches. Akihiro-san was behind the counter wearing his head scarf. Will and Yumiko were at the counter watching an episode of *Tora San* on the TV. Sanae busied herself bussing and cleaning tables.

"I wonder where Walt-san is right now?" said Yumiko.

"Probably at some train station somewhere," replied Will.

"baka," guessed Akihiro-san. "anna yatsuwa keemushoni itahooga, minnano tameda." ("We'd be better off if he was in jail.")

The door slid open and the noren popped up. "konnichiwa."

It was Itsuki. "konnichiwa," duoed Yumiko and Will.

"hai," ("Yes,") grunted Akihiro-san.

"amega furu rashiiyo." ("It's going to rain."), said Itsuki.

"hai."

"hoomuresuno hitotachiwa taihenda." ("Makes the homeless miserable.")

"sonotameni, seifuga boosui-shiitoo kubatterunjanai." ("That's why the government gives them tarps.")

"tokidoki jisatsuga aru tte yo." Sometimes there are suicides.") added Sanae.

That made everyone stop and consider for awhile. Akihiro-san scratched his chin. There had been a record number of suicides in Japan that year. Sanae wiped a table.

"Maybe he should get married," said Yumiko.

"Who?" said Will.

"Walt-san."

"Waruto-sanwa kekkonsuruto iinjyanaikashiratte ittandakedo." ("I said, 'Maybe Walt should get married,'") repeated Yumiko in Japanese to the others.

"anna yatsuto darega kekkon shitekureruka." ("No one would have him.") Said Ahihiro-san.

"dokashira? miboojindene amerikajinni attemitaitte yuu hito, shitteruwayo." ("I do know a widow who would like to meet an American, though,") volunteered Sanae-san.

"aitsu, kinoo itayo." ("I saw him yesterday,") said Itsuki.

Immediately everyone came to attention.

"What?" said Will, wondering what had been said.

"dooshite imamade damattetano?" ("Have you been holding out on us?")

"de, dokoni itano?" ("Where was he?")

"What?" asked Will again more insistently.

"He saw Walt," said Yumiko.

"I saw Waruto," said Itsuki.

"Tokyoodayo." ("I was up in Tokyo,") he continued in Japanese. "okyakusangane, keebano kippuo kuretanda." ("One of my customers had given me tickets to the horse races.")

"keeba? Waruto-san ga, keebajooni itano?" ("The races? Walt-san was at the horse races?")

"ee." ("Yes,") chuckled Itsuki, pleased with the attention he was getting. He waited until all eyes were focused on him. "sorede, zenzen hashirisoomonai umani, takusan kaneo kaketanda... dabanidayo. daremo sonnakoto shimasenyo." ("And he bet a lot of money on a real long shot. A dog of a horse. Nobody would bet on it.")

"baka," ("Stupid,") said Akihiro-san.

"nantekotoo..." ("Oh no,") said Yumiko. "kuyashigattadeshoo? ("Was he upset when he lost?")

"chigau, chigau." ("That's just it,") replied Itsuki. "kattanda." ("He won.")

"Eeeee???" ("WWWWhhhat???")

Yumiko quickly filled in the information for Will.

"sono umattenogane, saigomade hashirikireruka dookamo wakaranaiyoona umadattandakedo, kacchattanoyo. sonna kakuritsuwa 1000kaichuuni 1kkaittetokokashira." ("That horse looked like he wouldn't even last the whole race, let alone win it. But he did. The odds must have been a thousand to one.")

"That's great!" said Yumiko. "I am so happy for him."

"I knew he could do it," smiled Will.

Sanae looked up. "de, Waruto-sanwa dokoni ittano?" ("Where did he go?")

"saaaa." ("I don't know,") said Itsuki. "bokuwa maketande, moo iiyato omotte kaettekitanda. demo, Waruto-san, sono katta okanede, mata tsugino reesuni kaketamitai dayo. ("I lost, so I decided I'd had enough. But Walt went back to bet with the money he'd won.")

The faces dropped.

"Now what?" Will asked nervously.

"He bet more," said Yumiko in a hushed tone.

"Oh no," said Will. He sat back down.

"baka," said Akihiro-san.

Sanae was saddened. "dattara, zkekkyoku zenzen katanakattanomo onajijanai." ("It's like he had never won at all.")

"He is like an American Toro-san," said Yumiko looking back at the TV.

"He means well," said Will.

"Baka," added Akihiro-san.

Akio-san, the family farmer who had known Akihiro-san most of his life and was a regular at Hirota's slid the door open. "minna minna, Waruto-sanga kitayo. soremo, Tookyookara takushiini notte kitayo!" ("Hey everybody. Walt-san is here, and he came in a taxi all the way from Tokyo!")

Everyone scrambled to their feet and made for the door.

"minna matte!", ("Wait!") It was Yumiko. "moshikasuruto, Waruto-san, maeno koto, kimazuito omotterunjanaikashira? dakara, Waruto-san ga itemo, kinishitenai furi shiterunowa doo?" ("Maybe he is embarrassed about how he left. Perhaps we should pretend not to notice he's here.")

"un, sooshiyoo. minna, motono tokoroni modotte." ("Good idea. Everyone go back to where you were.")

Everyone went back to their original positions and pretended to be busy. Yumiko whispered the plan to Will.

Voices and shouts came from outside. Suddenly the door slid open and Walt stepped in followed by a small entourage of neighbors and shop keepers who had attached themselves to him. Walt sported an out of fashion brimmed hat and coat, and carried his small suitcase in one hand and a bag in another.

"Where is everybody?" he shouted.

"Oh, it's you." Will looked around nonchalantly. "You back?"

"You bet I'm back."

Just then the door opened and a taxi driver came in carrying a large bottle of sake.

"hai doomo. dokomade?"("Hello. Where to?")

"arigatoo." Walt took the bottle.

"Sake for everyone," said Walt. "We are celebrating. Here." He handed a small pouch full of money to Akio-san. "Pay the man, will you?"

Akio-san was a man of means, but his eyes widened when he saw all the money in the pouch. Walt had taken the taxi all the way from Tokyo, so the fee was substantial. Akio-san carefully counted out the amount for the trip. The driver turned to go.

"doraibaa-san," ("Driver") called Walt.

"hai?" ("Yes?")

Walt slipped another niman-yen into the driver's hand.

"nihon dewa chippuwa iranaindayo." ("Oh, we don't tip here,") said Akio-san reaching to stop him.

"iidesuyo, iidesuyo. sekkaku no gaijin san no gokooi nanode." ("That's okay. I don't like to offend foreigners,") said the driver. He snatched the money and vanished out the door.

"And now," said Walt, "a little trophy for the grizzled coot in the Willie Nelson bandana." He reached into the bag, and as he pulled it out he proclaimed, "A setoyaki chawan from Gifu Prefecture by way of Tokyo horses."

He pulled out a beautiful tea bowl with a green copper glaze and held it up for all to admire, smiling broadly.

Akihiro's eyes widened. He wiped his hands on his apron and came out for a closer look.

Walt looked at him and said. "sumimasendeshita." Then bowed.

Akihiro looked at him for a moment, then bowed back.

Walt, pleased to the brim with himself, bowed again. They both bowed again. Akihiro gingerly took the bowl.

"sugoi." He said. He examined it closely. Everyone gathered round, while Walt beamed.

Walt caught Will's eye. "You were wrong about the quarter million yen," he whispered. "It was more like half a million."

Akihiro-san carried the tea bowl to the glass counter, and put it in a place of honor. There it would rest for the next month for all his customers to see.

"Waruto-san, otanoshimiga aruyo." And now, young man, we have a surprise for you,") said Akihiro-san.

"Eh?" said Walt to Yumiko, "What did he say?"

"He said we are going to find you a nice wife."

"What?" Walt was not so sure he heard right. He thought it over. "A wife? Hmm. Well maybe. Maybe it is time for that."

Will was surprised. He had not thought Walt would go for it.

Walt thought out loud. "I would not ask for much. A man my age can't be too choosy."

"miboojin no Ayaka-sannandakedo, futari kodomoga irunone. Demo, sono kodomotachi mo moo ookikunattete, moosugu ieo derurashiino." ("The widow Ayaka has two children, but they are almost grown and will leave the nest soon,") said Sanae-san.

Walt continued his thoughts. "I don't ask for anything except that she is kind and gentle."

Will and Yumiko smiled and nodded. Others followed suit.

"However, nowadays a woman must hold a job as well as a man to make ends meet." He looked around.

"Of course, she may want to give me breakfast in bed on weekends----and a back rub now and then wouldn't be out of the question." Yumiko quietly translated what he was saying.

"Bringing me the newspaper and a cold can of beer would be good...especially if I'm watching a football game on TV. Micro waved snack food, of course, for an important game."

Faces around the room looked to Yumiko. She declined to translate.

Walt snapped out of the mood. "Who wants sake?"

Glasses and wooden cups came forward and were quickly filled. There were a few toasts of "kampai" from time to time, and Itsuki even tried to sing, "For He's a Jolly Good Fellow" but got off tune and couldn't remember how it ended.

"I learned a phrase of Japanese while I was away. A nice man at the horse-race park was very patient teaching it to me," boasted Walt. He tapped for silence and waited until he had everyone's attention.

Then, with a broad smile and terribly butchered Japanese he said, "kekkoo kedarake neko haidarake oshirino mawariwa kuso darake." ("Perfect is hairy, cats are full of ash, monkey bottoms are full of shit.")

Itsuki stood amazed, not quite sure how to react. Sanae-san giggled.

Yumiko frowned and stood up. "That is impolite, Walt-san. You talk like yakuza. You never say again."

Akihiro did not know what she had said. He decided that Walt had attempted to learn about Japanese culture and that it was an admirable thing to do.

"iijanaika, Waruto-san. Antano kedarakenekoni kampaida." ("Good for you, Walt-san. I drink to your hairy cats. kampai.") He raised his cup.

Akio-san raised his cup. "kedarake neko ni kampai." ("Hairy cats.")

Time wore on. The party evolved into something quieter and more reflective. The whole room seemed to be enveloped in a warm reverie. Akihiro-san admired the tea bowl and imagined himself serving the mayor at his next tea ceremony. The frog would probably appear to him for such an occasion, he decided. But it was too soon to tell.

Walt had consumed four or five glasses of sake and was beginning on another. He sat, teary eyed, imagining coming dutifully home to a "little woman" who would be waiting with dinner and slippers, smiling happily because he had returned home.

Will and Yumiko sat at the counter, Yumiko's head back against Will while she held two empty sake cups in her hands, softly, rhythmically beating them together.

The two customers had long gone, but their places had been taken by some of the shop people who had come in with Walt. No one ordered anything, no one indulged in anything other than alcohol.

Akio-san sat contently surveying the scene. He had gotten up three times and served himself a tall shochu with tea. He had known the Hirota clan since he had been in high school, and made a habit of staying in their lives. He often brought them produce from his farm, or fish he had caught on one of his many trips. Will had told him about the great fishing in Cabo San Lucas, Mexico—but Akio-san refused to fly in airplanes.

Akio-san smiled. His attention wandered until it fell on Yumiko's steady, soft clanking of glasses. He listened. The rhythm was slow, regular, unchanging. What had been unnoticed before seemed to draw him in now and became his main focus. He picked up a chopstick, and tapped his shochu glass. He found he could hit the glass in between the beats made by Yumiko. Occasionally he could improvise a couple of quick beats, and still fit into the tempo.

This went on for some time. Rain began to also tap its own beat lightly on the roof.

Walt, who had been sitting with a silly grin on his face, suddenly turned and looked at Akio-san, then turned back and looked at Yumiko still beating her sake cups. He slid off his stool and walked back towards the kitchen. He soon re-emerged grinning, holding two small bags one with rice, the other with dry azuki beans. He stepped out into the room and began to do a kind of dance, first putting one foot forward, then the other, shaking them and the bags in time with the music.

Akihiro-san noticed, and produced two dessert spoons. He began drumming on the top of the glass counter. One by one everyone in the room began to join in, softly at first but gradually building in volume and tempo. They beat on tables and counters, shaking their shoulders, and moving their heads with the beat, a crazy, spontaneous, uncharacteristic magical warp in time that rarely happens yet somehow magically does now and then. Akihiro-san played while never changing the seriousness of his expression, a far away look in his eyes. Others began to grin as they realized the uniqueness and absurdity of the situation.

Sanae hopped up and began dancing too. Itsuki soon joined, making strange sounds like a kabuki actor. After awhile as the noise grew and the rhythm became more and more irresistible a kind of conga line began to form and snake through the restaurant, participants exaggerating their movements and creating expressions on their faces that looked like the hurting joy of blues musicians. Some of the Japanese participants' movements evolved into a typical Japanese folk dance, lifting legs and arms in unison.

Outside the rain increased, gradually at first, then louder and louder until it poured down on the roof of the restaurant in a torrent. Will glanced up nervously at the roof, but others kept playing and dancing.

The noise built up and the dancing grew wilder. Suddenly through the window there came a blinding flash of light from a bolt of lightning hitting only blocks away, followed almost immediately by a deafening clap of thunder.

A gust of wind slammed into the room along with the thick wet smell of rain. A muffled, eerie cry grew in volume as Aka-chan ran in, her clothes and hair thoroughly drenched.

She slid to the middle of the floor on her knees trembling uncontrollably, her face contorted in agony.

"Bisakuga... denshani tobikondandatte!" ("Bisaku threw himself in front of a train!")

x x x x x x x x x x x x x x x x x x x x x x

"ohayo gozaimasu."

Itsuki slid the door open with his elbow and pushed his head through the nori, carrying his computer. What he saw stopped him short.

Akihiro-san and Walt sat side by side at the counter near the TV hunched over a computer. They took turns moving the cursor, grunting agreeably when something seemed to work right, and swearing intermittently in English or Japanese when it didn't.

It had been two weeks since the funeral for Bisaku, and Baby had not yet returned to work. Itsuki or Will and Yumiko would take leftovers every night in a plastic bag, and hang it on her doorknob at the Chateau Gotemba. Once Yumiko came across her in the bathing area downstairs. Baby had been alone in the bath. When Yumiko came she said "konnichiwa" but little else and left soon after.

George was in the Hirota kitchen making himself some eggs. He was supposed to meet Itsuki to work together but had his computer commandeered by the two older men. He had shown them how to search for branding irons and tea bowls, and now they were looking up square dancing in Japan.

Walt had just figured out how to run video of Japanese dancers decked out in elaborate square dance outfits. The women's dresses billowed outwards (except for those women who went as men and wore slacks instead). Most of the men had checkered shirts and a few had Stetson hats. The caller gave commands in English, and wore a fancy string tie with a polished stone like the ones Walt sometimes wore.

Akihiro-san watched the dancers on the screen. He grunted admiration and clapped Walt on the back.

"otoo-san," said Itsuki.

"urusaina. mireba wakarudaro, isogashiinda. (Can't you see I'm busy, numbskull?") Akihiro-san waved him away. Then he looked back at him and noticed he had his computer with him. He beckoned Itsuki over.

"nihongode yarerunoka? Mooo, kocchie mottekoi" ("Does that one do Japanese? Bring it over, idiot.")

Not long after that, Akihiro-san and Walt were straining and swearing over both computers while George and Itsuki sat at a table eating natto, eggs and rice and drinking tea. The Lazy Double R branding iron hung above Akihiro's grill, a place of honor since Walt had loaned it to him.

That night Akihiro-san uncharacteristically let Sanae-san close up the restaurant, while he and Walt went to a western concert where Japanese singers wore Stetson hats, played guitars and harmonicas and played western-style music. Walt was in heaven and Akihiro-san seemed to enjoy himself as well. Akihiro-san was even convinced to try on Walt's hat.

"Traditions must always be safe-guarded," they agreed. "Differences can be looked on with fear or as a source of deepening our appreciation of life. Everyone makes his own choice how to look at them."

The next evening Akihiro-san took a rare day off. He took Walt to see the Clydesdales and Budweiser wagon near the Horse Whisperer Restaurant. The owner came out and took them around to the jumping arena and introduced them to his daughter who had represented Japan in the Olympics. Then they went to Albert's bar (named for Frank Sinatra) and watched some horse jumping.

That evening back at Hirota's Walt introduced Texas Hold'em to Akihiro-san and some of the Gotemba locals. Will and Yumiko were there, as were Tsukamoto-sensei, Itsuki, George, Oryo, Sanae-san, and Fukumoto-san in his kimono.

After explaining the rules of the game Walt got into some of the strategy. Yumiko and George helped to translate. As Walt explained how to bluff an opponent, Yumiko stopped him.

"I can not do that," she explained. "I am a very honest person."

During the game later, however, she seemed to be okay with it. However, whenever she won a hand she would bow and apologize to the player(s) she had beaten.

She always forgot, and had to be reminded when it was her turn for the blind. "What if I don't want to bet this hand?"

"You still have to give the blind."

"Pain of neck," she would say.

After one hand Itsuki got very upset with his father. Itsuki had slightly raised after the flop, the turn, and finally after the river. Akihiro-san only called him each time, never raising. When they showed their hands he had a full house, Aces full of tens. Itsuki was angry that Akihiro-san had not raised him earlier, thus indicating he had a really good hand.

Akihiro-san, wearing his traditional head-band, looked dispassionately at his son.

"jinseitte kibishiimonda?"("Life is tough, isn't it?")

x x x x x x x x x x x x x x x x x x x x x

Early one August morning the little red Honda Civic pulled into the parking lot at Hirota's. Yumiko and Will dropped off a package that Walt had sent from California, a couple of mini-branding irons Akihiro-san could use on eel or whatever he fancied. They told Akihiro-san they would be taking a long trip around the southern part of Kyushu.

By lunch time they had already visited the gardens near Okayama. They went on to a castle, saw a statue of Momotaro (the peach boy), and drove up to the Midori Ryokan in Takahashi. They made their way up a steep mountain trail to the ghostly Matsu Bichu castle during a thunder and lightning storm but were too late to go inside.

The next day had them visiting a temple seen in a **Tora-san** episode, some samurai homes and then on to Iwakuni. That evening they dined aboard a small open boat near the Kintaikyo Bridge. It was a beautiful old bridge with steep arching spans that was once used by samurai who protected the Iwakuni Castle. In the old days, those not of samurai rank had to boat across as they were forbidden to use the bridge.

"Pain of neck," was Yumiko's comment.

After dinner their small boat chased along with other boats behind ukai, cormorant fishing boats. Those boats had a flaming torch on their prows. The usha or lead fisherman wore a kind of grass skirt (dangerously close to the flames in the bow), a dark kimono and kazaoriebashi (head band). He used large black cormorant birds that would dive down and catch ayu (small thin sweet fish). The birds had ropes around their necks that kept them from swallowing the fish.

Besides the brightness of the flame, a drummer would bang on a drum to attract the attention of the fish. It reminded Will of a story he once heard. A fisherman who had a beautiful new pole and reel promised a young boy he could have it at the end of the man's vacation if the boy would show him why he was so successful catching fish. The next day the boy took him to a spot on the edge of a lake and beat the water over and over with a stick. Far from scaring the fish, it drew them in with curiosity. The boy always had a long string of fish when he returned.

When the ukai got near, the usha would throw some of the catch into the tourist boats.

The next day Yumiko and Will retraced their route back north to visit Miyajima Island. Afterwards they headed for a hotel in Hiroshima.

x x x x x x x x x x x x x x x x x x x x x x

Early one August morning a little red Datsun pulled into the parking lot of the Shima Surgical Clinic. Dr. Hideo Fujimora had just spent time checking on Hugh Atkinson, a POW being held at the nearby Kempei-Tai Headquarters. The American, a radio operator from Seattle whose B-24J had come down near Hiroshima had attempted a few words of Japanese.

Now Dr. Fujimura began to collect his thoughts for a more demanding operation. He would be resetting several broken bones in the leg of a Japanese soldier that had not healed correctly because of an earlier hastily performed surgery.

As he entered the building he could hear the droning of two or three large bombers high in the air. He did not bother to look at them. There had been no air raids on Hiroshima during the entire war, and two or three planes would not mean a raid anyway. Instead he reviewed his patient's chart and then went to scrub his hands.

He did not realize that he was just minutes away from the first human event that would make Fujisan blink.

At the same time, only a block or two away, Eizo Nomura had gone down into the basement of a rest home where she worked. She was putting away some supplies that had come the day before and worked hurriedly so she could return upstairs to help.

Just down the road from the rest home, little Eichi Nozumo ate some fish and pickles. He got up from the table and headed for the door.

"Eichi,", said his mother. "mada gohanga nokotteruwayo." ("Come back and eat your rice.")

"Moo~..." ("Awww...")

"Zenbu tabetekaranishinasai." ("Finish your breakfast.")

Eichi broke for the door.

"chotto sokomade, ikkai ikudakedatteba. Sugu modorukara." ("Just going around the block once. I'll be right back.")

Before his mother could catch him, Eichi was off on his brother Junichi's bicycle. It was still too big for him. He had to push down hard on the pedals so they would come back up where he could reach them.

Eichi was hoping the bike would become his. Junichi would not need it any more. He was attending a military academy, and was paid well to help make ammunition for the war effort.

About 3 kilometers further away was Tsutomu Yamaguchi, visiting Hiroshima on ship building business from his hometown of Nagasaki. He was dressed in a western-styled suit and was hurrying to a breakfast meeting.

In the countryside was a group of American and English POW's, getting ready to go down into a mine. Jim Navas who had been part of a New Mexico unit that had been force marched in Bataan was hoping to bum a cigarette from his captors that August 6th, 1945.

The Enola Gay released Little Boy at approximately 8:14 AM. It dropped for almost a minute. The wind pushed it slightly past its original target, the Aiomi Bridge, and it detonated instead 600 feet directly above the Shima Surgical Clinic. Ninety percent of the physicians in Hiroshima that day were killed or seriously injured, including Dr. Fujimora who had been drying his hands when the shock wave hit. He evaporated.

A blinding flash was seen by Jim Navas, other POW's and their guards, soon followed by a jolt in the earth. Then came a deafening sound. A giant cloud rushed eleven thousand feet into the air. Jim had no idea what had happened. He felt it was the end of the earth.

Little Boy carried 130 pounds of uranium 235. Less than two percent of the material ignited, but the explosion was equal to 13 kilotons of TNT. A square mile was flattened, and almost 5 square miles destroyed by the blast and fire. Temperatures of over 7000° F melted glass and left only eerie silhouettes on walls of people unlucky enough to have been outside at the time. A blast of hot wind over 600 miles an hour slammed through Hiroshima, knocking down 2 out of 3 buildings throughout the entire city.

A bicycle was left mangled by the force and heat. A bowl of rice turned to charcoal. Watches stopped at 8:15. About 70 to 80,000 people were killed immediately. Others, marched like living dead, their arms held out in front of them to avoid the pain of seared skin rubbing against their sides as they walked to the river to cool themselves. There they would die, and their bodies would float down river, for days afterwards. Sometimes there were so many that the bodies dammed up the water.

Eventually two of every five people in Hiroshima that day would die. One of every seven of them were of Korean descent, in Hiroshima as war slaves.

Hugh Atkinson and the other American prisoners held at Kempei-Tai Headquarters died. Eichi Nozumo and his mother died. His brother Junichi, making ammunition, died. Dr. Fujimora died. Many people died years later from leukemia, cancer, malnutrition, or radiation sickness.

Although he was badly burned on his left side, Tsutomu Yamaguchi survived. He traveled back to his hometown of Nagasaki a day later and was in that city when it was bombed. He survived that, too. He did not die until 2010, a victim of cancer.

Eizo Nomura, who had been in the basement of a rest home only about 300 feet away from Shima Surgical Clinic, became the closest survivor to the epicenter of the bombing.

Another survivor damaged but still standing, was the dome of the Prefectural Industrial Promotional Hall, located between the intended bridge target and actual ground zero, about 500 feet away.

x x x x x x x x x x x x x x x x x x x x x x

Gembaku, the A Bomb Dome, as the Prefectural Industrial Promotional Hall is now called, was the first thing Yumiko and Will saw when they got off the bus at the Hiroshima Peace Memorial Park. They had left the car at the hotel because they knew there would be large crowds for the anniversary of the bomb that day.

The park was humming with activity. Anti-war and Peace banners were everywhere. A group of hare-Krishna's in pinkish-orange robes and tennis shoes danced and asked for money. Painters displayed their efforts, and petitioners asked everyone to sign for their cause (usually for world peace).

An old man who had been a survivor told a group of people around him that Americans never tell their children about the bomb and the effect it had. When Yumiko translated for him, Will recalled that his parents had told him about the bomb when he was quite young. He didn't doubt, though, that many Americans didn't tell their children about it.

"Hell," thought Will, "A lot of Americans don't know New Mexico is a state."

As they entered the park they saw a statue dedicated to Sadako Sasaki. She had been about two years old when the bomb hit. It wasn't until seven years later she was diagnosed with a disease caused by radiation.

The story goes that she was told if she folded a thousand paper cranes that she would survive. Dutifully she folded cranes, but as time went by the disease took its toll. She grew weaker and weaker. In 1955 she died having completed only 644 cranes. Schoolmates completed the rest of the thousand paper cranes for her.

Near her monument there was a case filled with paper cranes connected in long chains. All over the world (including in Will's Long Beach class) children had heard the story of Sadako and the thousand cranes, and learned how to make them. The folded cranes have become a symbol of peace, and a reminder of the long lasting effects of nuclear bombs.

Survivors of the bomb are called hibakusha (explosion affected people). There were more than 200,000 of them, some of them still suffering today from problems related to radiation. Koreans who were affected have finally been recognized through lawsuits they filed against the Japanese government. Like the victims of Hansen's disease, that recognition had been a long time in coming.

At precisely the time the bomb had detonated, a bell sounded over the packed park, followed by a minute of silence. Prime Minister Koizumi spoke, victims were recognized, pigeons released, a wreath was laid and a new museum was opened. Some of the Hiroshima Maidens who had gone to America for plastic surgery were there.

Yumiko and Will spent the rest of the day walking around the park, going into the museums, listening to accounts of eye-witnesses.

Back outside they bought some food from a vendor. There were people from all over the world. A high school girl walked up to Will and asked if she could interview him.

"Of course."

"You are American?"

"I am."

"How do you feel about the bomb?"

"I think it was a horrible thing."

"Do you think President Truman was a war criminal?"

"I think he did what he thought best."

"But there were thousands of innocent lives lost."

"Let me ask you something," said Will. "Have you ever heard of Pearl Harbor?"

"No."

"Do you know how many lives were lost in Nanking?"

"That's a place in China, isn't it? I don't know anything more."

Will looked at her and smiled. "I am glad to see you are practicing your English."

The girl smiled.

"I'm also glad that you are willing to get involved. It is your generation that need to know the dangers of atomic weapons."

The girl nodded.

"People are capable of great things when they put their minds to it. Look what Japan has done in India and Africa."

The girl seemed pleased.

"But people are also capable of doing horrible things. Which is why it's important to remember that we all have those possibilities within us."

He looked at her closely. "It is only when we know what we are truly capable of, for good and for evil, that we are free to make informed choices."

"Could I email you?" she asked.

"Of course, any time." Will scribbled his email and handed it to her.

"There was a wise man named Arthur Miller," he said. "He once said that we must look at the ugliness in our ourselves and embrace it like a horrible looking idiot child. It is only then we can accept ourselves and move on."

That evening, one could buy a raft and candle lantern for a small fee then write the name of someone who had perished in the bombing and launch the lantern from the bank of the river. The beautifully colored paper of the glowing lanterns would fill the water, like many of the souls that had floated down that river so many years earlier. After rounding the bend the lanterns were picked up and disposed of so as not to pollute the water.

Will bought a lantern. He wrote down the name of an uncle he never met, Ted Parker. Parker had been taken prisoner by the Japanese shortly after the war began. When the ship in which he and other prisoners were being transported came under bombing attack by American planes, he quickly organized the able-bodied prisoners to get ready to climb up the ladder to escape if the ship went down. The Japanese guard on deck fired three times down into the hold, then ran for his own life. The three bullets all hit Ted Parker, killing him.

Yumiko and Will climbed a small hill. They stood and watched as the lanterns floated slowly down the river. Ted Parker's floated along with the victims of the bomb.

Tomorrow they would head for Beppu and Yufuin.

# #

Tourists on the Hakone Ropeway might first notice their gondola swinging more than usual. The towers themselves may begin to sway, and the gondola cars slide off and plummet into the deep canyon below.

When Fujisan erupts, as it will, volcanic bombs will hurtle through the air for miles, becoming more bullet shaped before impacting. Even a small one could penetrate the roof of a car, as well as a skull. Larger ones, as big as a car and over 1000° Celsius would destroy anything in which they came in contact, traveling 600 meters from a vent from which they were thrown.

Gravel shaped pumice would collect along roads and on the roofs of buildings, gradually building up to hinder traffic and collapse structures. Deadly gases would permeate the air, concentrating in some areas more than others.

US Marines from Camp Fuji who trade off with the Japanese Defense forces in shelling the side of Mt. Fuji would find the mountain firing back at them.

Hakone visitors buying the blackened eggs that were to extend their lives by seven years would find their lives shortened by sympathetic eruptions going on in the surrounding Hakone hills.

A pyroclastic flow of tephra would travel faster than 450 miles per hour, hugging the ground and enveloping everything with which it came into contact. A victim taking a breath of the deadly hot gases would have his lungs seared into ash instantly and his melted insides turn to concrete.

The escape route through Hakone to the sea would be shut down, either by government edict, or by collapsed tunnels.

Fujisan would speak its own language. One all would hear, but only the mountain would understand. It would alter many, many lives. But it would not end all life.

In the meantime, natives and visitors carry on with their lives. School systems are run by those who did well in school, who are better at taking tests than making creative contributions to humanity.

Those in the shadow of the mountain endure great and minor struggles, dramas, and embarrassments, triumphs and comedies. They stress great importance on cultural differences, especially if their child is having trouble in class, or if a foreigner balks at the slowness of decision making or the meticulous details in bureaucracy.

Fortunately, there are real differences. For the enlightened they make life rich and interesting. The similarities of the human family are even stronger—from the gossiping and bickering, the competitiveness and the sense of failure that sometimes lead to needless tragedy, to the acts of compassion and love that are so often taken for granted.

Will and Yumiko would eventually move to California. Yumiko would write a cookbook and appear on local television. Will would return to teaching in California and become involved in the politics of the teachers' union. Eventually they would travel to Europe.

But that is another story.

Cast of characters

Aka-chan friend of Hirota family and worker at Hirota's (mother of high school student Bisaku)

Akio-san, early-70's, old friend of Hirota family, well to do gentleman farmer and fisherman

Ayla Michaela Mast, daughter of Will Mast by a previous marriage, 20 year old blond model

Bisaku, high school student nervous about exams (son of Aka-chan)

Fukumoto-san, fifties, old friend of the family, master wood craftsman and master of tea ceremony

George Olsen, late 20's, American from Alabama, married to Yumiko's niece, Oryo

Grandma Ruth Mast, (mother of Walt and Will Mast) who turned 91 the year Ayla Michaela's child was born in 2010

Hirota Akihiro, Early- 70's patriarch, owner of original Hirota's in Minami-Gotemba which he gave to his first son, Ryoma, then opened another unagi restaurant also called Hirota's in Gotemba. Master of tea ceremony, master of Bonkei, (Art on a Tray), and expert in koi, advocate for traditional Japanese customs.

Hirota Itsuki, mid-40's, youngest son—owner of Kinkabu I and II, drinking establishments

Hirota Ryoma, 50 eldest brother, owner of the original Hirota's in Minami-Gotemba

Oburo-san, 60's On the board for Nakamura Gakuen, lives near Hirota's where he was a regular patron

Oryo Olsen, daughter of Sanae, married to George Olsen, late 20's, with two small children—Mariko 7, and brother Hiroshi, 5

Sakai Tamatsu, Mayor of Susono, a town south of Gotemba

Sakurai Sanae (married name),early fifties, eldest daughter of Akihiro-san and older sister to Yumiko, divorced, with two grown and married daughters, cashier, waitress, bookkeeper at Hirota's in Gotemba. Accomplished at shodo (writing with a paint brush).

Suzuki Kentaro, president of a small, struggling company in the Ginza District of Tokyo

Tsukamoto Akira Sensei, Walt Mast's Japanese teaching partner at Nakamura Gakuen, kendo instructor, and involved in local civic events

Walt Mast, mid fifties, older brother to Will Mast, into traditional Western cowboy culture

Will Mast, mid-40's, divorced teacher from California, starting life in Japan at an immersion school (daughter Ayla Michaela Mast)

Yumiko Hirota Weeks, late 30's, slender proprietor of Yumiko's English School, and new wife of Will Mast

Nakamura Gakuen Administration Staff:

Dr. Chenoweth, late 40's, American (from Maryland), in charge of the English Immersion program

Dr. Nakamura, mid-70's, owner and head of all Nakamura schools

Teachers of immersion program for the Nakamura schools

Chauncy, 30's, flamboyant teacher/surfer from New York who has a love/hate affair with Japan.

Clyde Hasse, American teacher who has taught all over the world. Loves sumo matches and drinking beer.

Chateau Gotemba -- Modern (1980's?) Five sided condominium where Will and Yumiko Mast, and Aka-chan and her high school aged son, Bisaku live in Gotemba